TALENT GPS

A MANAGER'S GUIDE TO NAVIGATING THE EMPLOYEE DEVELOPMENT JOURNEY

RUSSELL; BAKER; HELT

authorHOUSE®

AuthorHouse™
1663 Liberty Drive
Bloomington, IN 47403
www.authorhouse.com
Phone: 1 (800) 839-8640

Published by AuthorHouse 04/26/2017

ISBN: 978-1-5246-8640-6 (sc)
ISBN: 978-1-5246-8639-0 (e)

Library of Congress Control Number: 2017904963

Print information available on the last page.

CONTENTS

PREFACE

As a manager, you know that a business is about making, buying, selling, or providing something to customers in exchange for money. Even public companies and not-for-profits must provide something in exchange for money in order to support the work done for their constituents. Like all managers, you frequently read reports that help you mitigate costs or bring in revenue. The success of the business you're part of is based on people like you managing the functional operations that will drive profit. The biggest cost in your organization is your employees. They're also the biggest asset in your organization—when they're chosen well, intentionally developed, and provided with career options. The business begins to fail if the wrong employees are chosen or the right employees are chosen but not developed. One of the most difficult and critical parts of your day-to-day job is to manage your team. The success of the business depends on how well you do this.

Managing your team well requires you as manager to monitor and tune key aspects of their time in the business including:

+ Hiring
+ Onboarding
+ Career Planning
+ Succession Planning
+ Retention
+ Engagement
+ Leaving the Business

Managing people is a full time job all on its own, but your job likely has many other functional areas like inventory, quality assessment, engineering, manufacturing, project management, and a myriad of other processes that drive effective business growth. It's hard to spend enough time on managing people when daily emergencies need you. Tactical day-to-day problems can eat up time that should be spent on strategically growing your team. Having a stable, scalable process to manage people would make it more possible to pay attention to managing your staff. We intend to give you that process in this book.

Since the economy improved, the word *talent* has come up more often in business. *Merriam-Webster's Dictionary* defines talent as "a special ability that allows someone to do something well." In this book, we're using the word talent to represent the people you supervise and lead at work. Each person in combination with other members of the team uses their talent to improve the business. Your job is to keep the talent connected and engaged so that they stay in the organization. This isn't easy. When the economy is sluggish, a manager must focus on scaling the team down while keeping the best employees. Cutting too many people puts the business at risk, as does keeping too many. Once the fateful decisions are implemented, exhausted managers may neglect the engagement of employees, assuming the workers are grateful to still have a job. Hard times require communication and encouragement, even when the manager does not feel like doing that.

In a stronger economy, managers must scale up to hire and onboard new employees quickly. Whether in good or bad economic times, each hire is critical to the future of the company. Managers know this well and feel the pressure of these decisions. For many, hiring feels like a stressful crapshoot. In addition to other aspects of your increasingly busy job, you still have to focus on employee growth and engagement to keep the best team members.

We Believe:

Brittney, Michelle, and I returned from the recent international ATD (Association of Talent Development) conference with a new perspective about talent. The association used to be focused on learning and development (you may call this training) and is clearly moving to be a force in the talent arena where we believe learning and development is a subset. We share the same passions:

- Learning and development is about growing people and performance. All three of us love doing this. However, it only works when it's part of a strategic workforce strategy and vision. To separate learning and development from talent development is like splitting up a family. They each contribute different value to the same purpose: grow people.
- As a manager, your HR department may focus on the legal aspects of HR and not be staffed to grow talent. Like your peers, you may find you have the responsibility for growing talent without HR and without the background needed.
- Every time one of us writes about talent, we're mindful that talent is made up of real people who work, have people who care about them and are trying to get along in the world they're in. For the three of us, our calling is to help people go from where they are to where they want to go in their careers. This is what talent means to us. As a manager, we hope you share this vision.
- When talent is made up of complex processes and cumbersome technology, managers are going to have difficulty finding time to get it all done. In this book, we're suggesting a simplified, repeatable process that will be scalable and clear to everyone involved. Each worker is worried about his or her job. Our goal is to make the process explicit and reduce the worry of the unknown. If people are on the same page and talking to each other, processes become simple. If people aren't on the same page or talking to each other, no process will save you.
- Brittney Helt and I have experience cooking down complex processes and growing performance. Michelle Baker is an experienced Talent Development leader gifted at creating purposeful processes that grow talent. Nice meeting you.
- Talent Development has parallel steps throughout a career. Onboarding isn't just for new hires; it's also for new promotions. We believe onboarding is necessary in many parts of the process, even after learning and development. Without onboarding, knowledge

doesn't transfer to performance. Succession Planning is a variation of Career Planning—you can't get a new job if no one is ready to replace you. This awareness helps to simplify the process.

• People don't work forever. Everyone will leave the company at some point. The process has to include this reality. We also believe that there are people who don't want to climb the corporate ladder. It was important to us to integrate "Stay" points within the process. At any time, it's okay to not want to go to any other job.

Why GPS?

A career can't be mapped to one predictable path. Opportunities change, bosses change, companies merge and the future moves. It's like using a GPS to get somewhere—sometimes the route is straightforward. When it isn't, the GPS knows where traffic is and can reroute you. Sometimes your GPS goes a little crazy and sends you in circles. Sometimes careers don't go the way we'd planned.

Both with GPS and careers, managers have to keep their eyes open, know where North, South, East, and West are, and use judgement to help staff navigate current and future work. Careers are a process, not a project. A critical role for the manager is to revisit goals as part of career planning to adapt to changing realities.

How to Navigate this Book:

There are seven chapters in this book providing you with tools and tips to navigate the process modelled above:

Engagement and Accountability: Keeping great employees is only possible when they are engaged and accountable in the current job. Every person you manage at every point in their career needs reinforcement to remain engaged and accountable.

Hiring: Unconscious Bias is the enemy of hiring, and we are all biased. Ryan Holmes, CEO of HootSuite, has said that "one subpar employee can throw an entire department into disarray. Team members end up investing their own time into training someone who has no future with the company."

There's a serious cost to hiring the wrong person:

- From Robert Half International https://www.entrepreneur.com/article/244730 CFO survey – bad hires cost productivity, 11% said bad hires reduce sales, supervisors spend 17% of their time (1 day/week) managing poorly performing employees). Final estimate: Thousands of dollars.
- The Department of Labor estimates that the cost of a bad hire = 30% of the employee's potential first-year earnings.
- The rest of the team gets dissatisfied with your attention on the bad hire.
- The average new hire turnover is 23%, compared with 16% for all employees https://www.thestreet.com/story/12243638/1/the-real-cost-of-a-bad-hire.html

As manager, you don't have time or budget to replace a new hire that isn't working out. That's what makes hiring so intimidating. We'll share automated tools to create a Job Benchmark to increase the odds that your hire matches your job taking the bias out of it.

Onboarding: Any time an individual goes into a new position, they need onboarding. Whether it's when they are hired, promoted or moved laterally. Onboarding simply means a transition plan including training and coaching preparing them for their new responsibilities.

Career Mapping: Each employee has personal goals and dreams. Most know vaguely where they'd like their career to go. When you, as Manager, help people create a map to achievement, you drive engagement and retention. It's also your responsibility to work with them to revisit and adjust the map as the world, the business, and individuals change.

Promotion: Promotion is a variation of hiring. The same unbiased tools you'll learn about in the Hiring chapter will also help you in the Promotion chapter.

Succession Plans: Succession Plans are a variation of Career Mapping with one significant addition. To be promoted and succeed to the next level, someone must be ready to replace you in your current job. As manager, you must build a clear expectation for all your team that they are responsible for growing the person who will replace them.

We wrote this book, so you can skip straight to the chapter you need. Each chapter will have stories of good and bad implementations, process, tools and techniques. Each template and tool is detailed in Appendix D, and you'll be referred there in chapters when these are discussed. There is a link in Appendix F which will take you to our download site.

There are two versions of tools available for you to drive the Talent GPS process: paper-based and online diagnostic tools. Here's how the tools compare:

TYPE of TOOL	Strength	Shortcoming	Price
Paper Based Tools	• Included in the book as PDFs • Easily distributed to all supervisors and team members • Can be adjusted to meet the needs of your organization	• Manual Job Benchmarks are very time consuming and less accurate • Requires documentation storage standards	Free, labor costs only
Virtual Diagnostic Tools	• Samples are in the appendix, available from russellmartin.com • Virtual and very compliant • Gap Reports for Job Benchmarks don't have to be done manually	• May not align with the standard assessments you are currently using • Requires documentation storage standards • For sale, not free (volume discounts available)	Priced depends on the tool being used $ 150 – 350 per person on average

Regardless of the type of tool you choose, **all talent tools are private information about a person and must be kept private.**

Please feel free to contact us at any time at info@russellmartin.com with any questions. Thank you so much for joining this journey with us.

Special thanks to the following:

Michelle Baker and Brittney Helt, co-authors who gracefully rolled with the punches during this writing project. Both are gifted Talent Development gurus and I appreciate very much their friendship and brains.

Nate Redman, author-by-calling, for stellar emergency editing.

Chad Musellman for adding his fun voice to our cover and writing chunks. Never underestimate the secret side of an IT Professional.

Keely McGrath for keeping the world at bay while I push this book out the door.

Ty and Paula Moser for their support and partnership.

Cat Russo and Jacki Edlund-Braun for helping us with our book concept and base while in very challenging circumstances.

All the friends who supplied testimonials for this book (see back cover and inside)

Author House for teaching me how to self-publish. Watch out world, here come more books!!!

As always, thanks to my supportive and loving family: Doug, Kelly, Katherine and Kristin.

Thanks to the ATD community and L&D friends who continue to fight the battle against bad training and lack of performance. Your support is my rock.

"The work you do is sacred. Be careful messing with someone else's life." - Lou Russell

Chapter 1

Calculating Best Route: Building A Process to Improve Engagement and Impact through the Employee Life Cycle

"If you expect an employee to be loyal and stay with you, you've got to give them something worth sticking around for." –Brittney Helt

"The median number of years that wage and salary workers had been with their current employer was 4.2 years in January 2016, down from 4.6 years in January 2014, the U.S. Bureau of Labor Statistics reported today." – www.tenure.pdf, Bureau of Labor Statistics U.S. Department of Labor.

The business world isn't what it used to be. Gone are the days when the majority of people were hired for a specific job, clocked in at 9am and clocked out at 5pm. Gone are the days when it's expected that someone will stay in one job for the majority of their adult life. Gone are the days when a manager could assume that once a hire was made, the job would be filled for the next 15 years.

It's not an easy market. Today, the good candidates already have a solid position. The great candidates are sought after and courted by several organizations. It's expected that professionals will hold a role for a few years, not a few decades. The current job market is a jungle and recruiters and managers are constantly battling to attract and retain the best employees possible. The million-dollar question is, "How do you retain the best?" There's no magic wand—sorry. **But there is hope.**

Navigating Careers

A young college graduate entered the workforce a month after the recession hit in 2008. Her degree was basically a formality—unrelated to any industry in which she planned to job-hunt. Like many people in that moment this young lady, who we'll call Beth, found herself without a purpose, without a plan, and without a job. Thanks to the tough economic climate at that time, though, she also found herself, like many Millennials, open to new possibilities.

Beth was introduced to a company that was on the brink of a rebuild. Their CEO was looking to grow the organization after a rough few years and was searching for a project manager with many of the strengths Beth brought to the table. Looking at the job market, Beth thought "What the heck!" and jumped into the world of learning and development. This was a long way from her degree in telecommunications, and a subject she knew nothing about, but Beth was lucky enough to have a mentor willing to invest in her growth.

Beth settled into her role as project manager and grew to love the industry. After a few years as a project manager, she was given the opportunity to learn more about the organization from the business development side of things. A few years after that, she was challenged to take more opportunities in front of customers and clients. After seven years in the field, she's totally immersed in every aspect of the business and completely engaged in the industry.

Seven years. And let's not forget—she's a Millennial. A recent statistic showed that the average tenure of a Millennial in a specific work role is two years, and Millennials consider themselves loyal after giving an organization seven months of time. So, what is it that's made Beth such an outlier?

- **Impact.** Since beginning work with her organization, she's been shown exactly how her role contributes to the overall success of the organization. She knows that what she does has an impact, and that gives her purpose.

+ **Communication.** Expectations have been openly and honestly communicated to Beth. When she finds herself in doubt or rethinking her path, there's trust built into her relationships that allows her to openly discuss next steps and any potential problems or issues coming down the path.

+ **Feedback.** Feedback is given often and in both directions. Very early in her career Beth was given a voice and encouraged to give open and honest feedback. That's very empowering and very effective.

+ **Investment.** The owner, the employees, the facilitators, and the industry all invest and highly value their people. Each team member knows without a doubt that they're uniquely important to the organization. Beth knows the more she invests in herself and the success of the organization, the better the company functions. Among other things, that gives her a sense of pride and belonging. Beth is excited to see where the company goes next and is happy to think of the personal impact she'll have over the next five to ten years.

Goals of the Chapter

In this chapter, you'll be challenged to start thinking about the process you use with your employees from hire to retire, which includes:

+ Establishing a reality for the current work world, your team, and your current organization

+ Creating a communication plan that will encourage engagement throughout the entire career lifecycle of each person who reports to you.

+ Outlining a flexible process that will live and evolve through the entire career cycle of your employees

+ Choosing tools and guidelines to help you move your employees through the process, decreasing bias, and increasing communication and engagement with your employee

In the following chapters, you'll learn that many managers and supervisors are struggling to map a route for their employees that works well from the time they've hired the right person until that person retires. Two common challenges arise:

1. Engagement: employees feel good about their role and therefore give to it all their effort and attention during most of the time they're "working."
2. Talent: employees meet the competencies and roles required of the job as well as the cultural fit of the organization. Roles are changing and so are candidates—it's hard to find a good fit.

In many cases these two things are discussed separately. If that's you, stop immediately. Think about it: if an organization can find the right fit for the right role, engagement will increase. Keeping your employees happy, growing, and engaged increases the likelihood they won't get bored and they'll continue to grow and build their roles within your organization. The key is keeping both engagement and talent in mind in each decision during the lifecycle of a person's career by creating a simple, clear, and cohesive process. Both challenges we've discussed can be met by strategically aligning your team members with their roles and building a process that all employees can follow during their tenure.

Take a moment to think about the current reality within your organization. Later in the book, you'll find a detailed worksheet to plan your career. Start now by thinking about its potential ideal state. What are ways you and your organization can bridge the gap between reality and an ideal state? Use the table on the next page as an example.

Reality	Gap	Ideal
I tell prospective employees they're great candidates with lots of potential and that they'll "go far" in this organization, but I don't give proof to support those statements to others.	Begin filling this gap by putting quarterly meetings on the schedule for my direct reports to discuss options and a plan.	A plan is mapped out that allows me to share with my team member where they can grow within our organization and the steps required to achieve that goal.
	Ask my direct reports to build a reality v. ideal state to share with me and work together to bridge those gaps.	

Starting Point. In our Talent GPS diagram you saw in the Preface, there's no end—it's a continuous process. An employee either stays or retires. You may be wondering: who owns this process? Many will jump to the obvious answer—Human Resources (HR). Not so fast. While HR can play an important role in the success and progress of employees, the importance of engagement with you—their manager—shouldn't be overlooked. It's easy to believe the only person responsible for your employee's happiness and success is your employee—and in many areas of a job this is true. But don't ignore the fact that part of the success and happiness of your employee(s) is dependent on their relationships within the workplace—i.e. their relationship with you. It matters. A lot. Who wants to have a horrible relationship with their manager or supervisor? No one. It's likely you may be accountable for your employees' work product, even if they're responsible for it. It's imperative that the relationship between you and each of your employees is clearly established and respected to ensure that engaged employees are producing successful work.

Before discussing what to do, let's define a few terms that are very important to this chapter and to beginning your journey.

Engagement: This is a buzzword that's thrown around a lot when discussing careers. For our purposes, engagement refers to someone being "all-in"—a person is committed to their craft, involved in all aspects of their role, brings ideas to the table, and plays an active part in their career journey.

Accountability: In this case, we're talking about having the authority to accept responsibility for yours or someone else's actions. In the career journey you may often be accountable for others' successes as well as your own.

Responsibility: Think of this as the next level in accountability. When you're responsible, you own your decisions and have the authority to choose the correct path for that task or decision. In some cases, your supervisor or manager may be the one held accountable, but you're the one who's responsible.

There are two key needs your employees have:

1. Clarity around the purpose of their work. *Why am I doing this?*
2. Ability to measure and make an impact. *Does what I do matter?*

When you and your organization recognize this, it's an important step in investing in the growth and engagement of your employees. Think about ways you're supporting your employees in fulfilling these needs. It starts from the time you post a position until that employee's time with you is complete. What are some things your leader does or could do that would make you take notice? Are any of those things you could implement with your own employees?

In the new "normal" work life most people (from individual contributors all the way to the top tier of leadership) are addicted to juggling multiple

> Take a moment to make a list of things that if done for you would help you feel appreciated and valued. Next to each item, jot down an idea of how you can translate this into something valuable for your employee(s).

projects, multiple processes, and multiple tasks. Employees pride themselves on cramming as many meetings and tasks as possible into a single day. Communication technology has improved, but research suggests communication is impossible to do well while multi-tasking. Knowing that you're multi-tasking and that your employees are multi-tasking should trigger a red flag when it comes time to communicate. Take care to stop and have intentional communication through the entire life cycle of each of your employees' careers. Build a communication plan to help guide the conversation through each leg of the career journey. Here's a list of different times you may identify the need for intentional communications with your employee. Take time now to work on a communication plan to help address different conversations that can help build trust and appreciation.

+ Job Posting
+ Interview
+ Onboarding
+ Employee Development (annual performance review, quarterly performance check-in)
+ Succession Planning

It's a process. Think about your current method for hiring and retaining talent. Do you struggle to keep employees engaged? Do you talk to them about their role and their path? What happens when an employee moves on or moves into a new position? Do they get additional onboarding sessions to help guide them in the right direction?

The talent engagement process should be just that—not an event but a process. The word "talent" might sound impersonal or abstract, but think about talent as something very personal and the most important resource your organization can have. When one of your employees is having issues or concerns over their career path, it's impacting their lives. It's no secret that when you have to make the tough decisions about a person's future in their career, you're also making a huge impact on their life. They take what you say and the decision you've made home with them to their family. This makes it even more important to stay active throughout their entire career path to help keep the lines of communication open and the engagement high.

Building a talent roadmap to guide your employees also helps guide a conversation with employees who may not want to take the traditional route. Below is a typical career path for the Learning & Development field:

Training Coordinator > Training Specialist > Instructional Designer > Learning Facilitator > Learning Manager > VP of Learning > Chief Learning Officer

What happens when one of your employees decides they don't want to follow the traditional path? While it may seem there's a clear and direct path to "success," as a manager, it's important to remember that that path is unique for each person. While you may enjoy your interactions leading a team, you may have an individual contributor who has no desire to lead anyone. Instead of following the traditional career path that you, your predecessor, HR, or the leadership team has laid out, take the time to understand what success means, looks like, and feels like for your employees. A great tool for doing this is a Career Map. This is different from a Career Plan—there's not a right and wrong path, rather a Career Map gives space for alternate routes, slow drivers, and delays. In Chapter Four, Career Maps are discussed in more detail, but for now, the important things to remember when thinking about your employees and their paths are:

- Not everyone takes the same path—giving employees room to grow and change their minds is important.
- Your definition of the path to success may be vastly different from that of your co-worker, boss, or employee—and that's okay.
- Implementing and creating a Career Map (See Appendix D and Chapter 4) can be an uplifting and enlightening experience. Take the time to discuss this with your employee(s) and ask them to complete their own. Block out dedicated time to do this exercise yourself to demonstrate just how important this is to your team and encourage each of them to do the same.

Once an employee has created a Career Map and has their individual plan, it's time to start considering the next steps. Over the last several years, Succession Planning has been something of an afterthought, most certainly not a priority. As you've likely guessed from the high-level look you've already had at the Talent GPS process, it's important to continue to include your employee in the conversations surrounding their next move. It's clear that moving one of your employees to another job leaves a hole in your team, which can cause disruption. Encourage your employees to be ready to replace themselves. You'll learn more about this in Chapter 6. For now, it's essential to remember that the Career Map that was created earlier in the process informs and builds into the Succession Plan.

It's easy to see how important building on the process and following that process through the entire lifecycle can be. One challenge you may still be thinking about is how to implement all of this. In the remaining chapters, you'll be able to practice with different tools and templates and take those to your employees to help open the lines of communication and foster engagement and empowerment in your team.

TTI Talent Insights TriMetrix Assessment Suite®

In our practice, we prefer to use a tool to help prevent bias and allow the candidate to reference their report and progress through the entire process. The TriMetrix assessment measures the candidate's Behaviors (what they do), their Motivators (what drives them to action or the why), their Acumen (world view), and their Competencies (skills). (Refer to Appendix B for samples of these powerful tools.) Each candidate completes this assessment, along with an Emotional Quotient assessment during the hiring process. Their results follow them throughout their career to help inform each area of the overall process. In each of the following chapters, you'll learn more specifically about how this tool is used. If you have an assessment tool you already use, you'll also learn ways to adapt your tool to work in each area of the process. To learn more about the TTI Success Insights Assessment Suite®, contact info@russellmartin.com . If you do not have assessments or the budget to get them, we have also included paper worksheets in Appendix D.

What happens if you skip this?

Without an engaged and loyal workforce, organizations will experience high turnover and will be forced to focus on finding new candidates, instead of growing and maintaining those they already have. Turnover is expensive. Recent studies suggest it costs up to three times the salary of an employee to find, replace, hire, and train a new employee. Wouldn't you rather use that money in your budget on something else?

Lessons Learned

- When creating a career engagement process, instead of an event, multiple opportunities to discuss progress and receive feedback build a two-way path for communication, allowing the employee to feel more engaged and to feel more ownership of their career destination.
- Building a career process should involve the employee. When an employee takes ownership of their own destiny they're more engaged and more likely to follow the designated path that's been agreed upon by both the organization and the employee.
- Using tools, such as assessments, to help in the process eliminates bias and provides proof to the employee of development and involvement opportunities.

Chapter 2

Hiring with Intention: Right Person, Right Place, Right Way

"The real work environment must meet or exceed the expectations set during the interview process, or your incoming employee's experience will always be lacking in trust." - Michelle Baker

Navigating People

Imagine this scenario: an intelligent, motivated professional applies for a position with a seemingly progressive organization. Knowing the job market is competitive for hiring top talent, this company has done an excellent job branding themselves as an exciting place to work and grow a career. During the interview process, the young professional is impressed by the company's core values, friendly interviewing team, and attractive benefits (Ping-Pong tables! Free snacks! Affordable healthcare plans!), ultimately accepting what seems to be a competitive offer for a terrific career opportunity.

Unfortunately, when he reports for work, it's immediately apparent that the reality is much different than the blissful picture painted during the interview process. Job responsibilities are far beyond the scope of what was originally discussed, communication is lacking, and there's no onboarding plan in place to help build a connection to the organization. Disappointed and left to fend for himself with few resources and little direction, the professional never creates a solid bond with the new company. He likely continued to explore other job options, or possibly worse: he "quit mentally, but stayed physically" with the organization, performing at a lower, less productive level and failing to achieve his career goals or organizational potential.

Sadly, this scenario is all too common for new employees of organizations in all industries. Perhaps you've experienced a similar situation firsthand during your career. Talented, intelligent, newly-hired professionals of all experience levels—from recent college graduates to seasoned leaders—find themselves wandering on a confusing path through the hiring process.

Chapter Goals

In your role as a manager, hiring new employees is a critical component of leading others and developing an effective, engaged team. How are you taking ownership of it? In this chapter, you'll explore:

- A manager's role in the hiring process
- How managers can build partnerships with other hiring stakeholders
- Tips for conducting successful, informative interviews
- Key accountabilities and other deliverables for matching the ideal candidate for the job

Whether you've hired new employees in the past, you're expanding your team for the first time, or you're looking to backfill a position for an employee who's leaving the organization, this chapter will prepare you to hire your newest team members with confidence and intention.

The Journey Begins with a Job Description

If this book is to serve as your GPS for developing employees, then crafting a clear, concise job description is your route's starting point. A job description defines the job title, essential skills, responsibilities, and qualities for the role. It also serves as the foundation for the relationship between an employee, you as the manager, and the organization. It's imperative that the job description be accurate, appropriately worded, and that it sets clear expectations for job performance, not only during the interview and onboarding period, but throughout an employee's tenure in the role. When performance or discipline issues occur, the job description is your reference to benchmark the employee's performance and actions against the expectations that have been communicated. It can also be used to assess superior performance—perhaps an employee consistently performs at a level much higher than outlined in the job description—it's important that you benchmark those successes as well!

RecruitLoop.com lists 5 helpful steps to writing a concise job description:

1. Specify an accurate job title that reflects the true nature of the job and duties being performed.
2. List the job duties and responsibilities associated with the role, including the expected percentage of time spent focused on those duties.
3. Clarify specific skills the employee will demonstrate on the job, as well as organizational behaviors, traits, or competencies that are essential for the role or organization.
4. Pinpoint key relationships, including the reporting structure and hierarchy of the role within the organization.
5. Identify a salary range that is competitive and aligns with the role, education, and experience level required for the position, as well as with your organization, industry, and demographic.

While the creation of a job description format or template may be the responsibility of your Human Resources department, it's your obligation to ensure that a job description is kept updated and accurately outlines the position. After all, as the manager, you know the team better than anyone else, right? As new leaders, organizational priorities, mergers and acquisitions, and other job-altering events occur, job responsibilities often shift. The job description should outline the role as it's being filled now, not a decade ago or whenever the role was originally created.

As you're looking to fill a role—whether through internal or external hiring, carefully review the job description on file and ask yourself these questions:

+ What purpose does this role fill on my team and within the organization?

- How does this role impact or interact with our customers, organization, and industry?
- What are the MUST-HAVE skills, experiences, and competencies for an employee to be successful in this role?
- What are the important, but less critical, skills, experiences, and competencies that would be helpful for an employee to be successful in this role? (These are your NICE-TO-HAVES!)
- When was the last time the job description for this role was updated?

By answering these questions, you'll be able to thoroughly audit your job descriptions and ensure you've defined what's necessary or desirable for a successful employee.

It's more than just the job description

Hiring is about making sure that the best person fits the job. Below are the important deliverables required for effective job matching.

Developing Key Accountabilities: Create 3-5 statements explaining what the job must deliver for the organization to thrive. These statements are reflections of specific actions, not competencies. To ensure that an accurate reflection of job actions is created, this should be done by a small group of Subject Matter Experts who perform the job or interact closely with that role, ideally with no more than 10 people involved. Once the Key Accountabilities are created, rank them in order of importance and indicate the percentage of time spent focused on that function on the job. This will help you in the interview and candidate selection process. You'll find an example of Key Accountabilities in Appendix D Templates and Worksheets)

Job Benchmark: The next step of the process, based on the Key Accountabilities, is to establish a Job Benchmark. Once the Subject Matter Experts agree on the Key Accountabilities, they complete a questionnaire about the job—behaviors, motivators, acumen, and competencies/skills. After completion, all answers are combined for comparison about the role itself, without a specific person or candidate in mind. Additionally, the Job Benchmark tool will produce interview questions based on the ideal role—you can use a gap report to focus your questioning around strengths, gaps and other insightful factors.

Gap Report: Finally, once you have candidates in mind for the position, they complete a similar questionnaire. This is used to compare each candidate against the Key Accountabilities and Job Benchmarks to identify which candidates best meet the necessary criteria for the role. As you measure this, consider:

+ Which candidates possess the necessary skills?
+ Where are the gaps?
+ What can be coached or trained?
+ What qualities *cannot* be coached or trained?

It's important to note that this shouldn't be the only thing you do to interview and measure candidates. This process should be used in conjunction with a solid interviewing process, led by your HR/Talent Acquisition partners. (To learn more about the TTi Trimetrix® tools, please visit Appendix B Diagnostic Assessments for explanations and sample reports.)

Clarify Expectations Upfront

Once a job description has been created and key accountabilities have been defined, it can be used to help clarify expectations with your partners in the recruiting and hiring process. For them to help you seek out qualified, talented candidates, it's important for them to understand exactly what you're looking for!

A comforting thing to remember is that you're (hopefully!) not alone in the hiring process. There are several stakeholders with whom you should be communicating as you seek and select a new employee. Those partners may include:

+ Your Human Resources/Talent Acquisition (recruiting) partners
+ Your direct supervisor
+ Your department/division leader
+ Your existing direct reports/team members

- Other stakeholders who have influence over hiring decisions
- Candidates, and ultimately your selected incumbent for the position

Establishing and maintaining open communication with these partners will help you clarify expectations for a new employee, including:

- The need for the role itself
- Job Title
- Desired education and experience level
- Salary Range
- Key Responsibilities
- Work schedule and arrangements—office hours, working from home, flexible schedule, etc.
- Travel requirements
- Desired start-date

With a variety of partners involved in recruiting and hiring, who truly "owns" the process? Your Human Resources department, specifically the Talent Acquisition/Recruiting team, might lead the process for your organization, but their purpose is to support the business (you!). Since screening, interviewing, and hiring talent is their primary focus—and they've seen a lot—it's worthwhile to listen to their input and consider their advice. However, as the manager, you're the one held accountable for a successful (or not-so-successful) hire. Regardless of how busy you and your stakeholders are, be firm in your stance to seek out and hire the best, most qualified candidate for the position, even if it takes a little longer. Ultimately, a bad hiring decision costs an organization dearly. According to a 2013 survey by CareerBuilder, more than half of those who responded said they have "felt the effects of hiring someone who turned out to be a poor fit for the job or did not perform it well." 41% of those surveyed said that a bad hire has cost them at least $25,000. Ouch. Other business factors impacted by a bad hiring decision could include: lower productivity, cost of time spent recruiting and training a replacement, reduced employee morale, or even a negative impact on the customer experience.

It shouldn't take a survey to teach you that bad hiring decisions result in a negative impact on your business. However, the same CareerBuilder survey asked why bad hiring decisions happen. The results may surprise you:

- 38% said the company needed to fill the position quickly. (Ah, the old "just get a warm body in here—we'll train them" strategy.)
- 34% said, "It just didn't work out." (Unfortunately, this happens sometimes—even with qualified, talented candidates.)
- 21% said the company didn't test or research the employee's skills well enough. (Anyone can create a beautiful resume or give a winning interview—but can they back it up?)
- 11% said the company didn't perform adequate reference checks. (Will someone else verify their experience? If not, that's a warning sign!)

The lesson here, dear manager? Take full responsibility for the outcome of every hiring decision—it will only strengthen your influence as a leader and help you learn for future hiring endeavors.

Simplify the Process

The interview process is a tremendous learning experience for a manager. To make an informed hiring decision, fully engage yourself in the recruiting and interview process. Your HR/Talent Acquisition partners will appreciate your involvement, as it allows them to tailor recruiting efforts and zero in on exactly what you are seeking.

While organizations' internal processes vary, the interview process is often broken into three primary stages:

1. Initial phone screen interviews
2. First-round face-to-face interviews
3. Second interviews for final candidates

Each stage is important and serves a unique purpose in making a successful hiring decision:

Stage	Purpose
Initial phone screen interviews	A brief phone interview, typically led by an HR/Talent Acquisition representative. Basic questions are asked to verify background information, qualifications, and determine whether the application would be a possible fit for the role and worth investing time for a face-to-face interview.
First-round face-to-face interviews	Once potential candidates have been identified through the phone screening process, they're questioned by one or more interviewers to determine which candidates are most qualified and the best possible fit for the job.
Second/final interviews for final candidates	When it's necessary to further assess or compare final candidates, a second meeting is scheduled. These interviews often include work simulations, case studies, or discussions of specific issues. These methods help pinpoint desirable behaviors and qualifications that assist the final hiring decision.

Preparing to Lead a Face-to-Face Interview

Once your HR/Talent Acquisition partner has completed initial phone interviews, s/he will work with you to begin scheduling face-to-face interviews. It's surprising how many managers simply rely on a recommendation from their HR/Talent Acquisition partner, and show up for a face-to-face interview with little to no preparation or understanding of the candidate. A simple 5-minute scan of the resume prior to the scheduled interview isn't a sufficient hiring strategy. The old expression, "an ounce of prevention is worth a pound of cure," is smart advice for any manager when faced with interviewing a potential candidate. Here are a few guidelines to prepare for the interview process:

+ Review each application and resume in advance, and again immediately before the interview, particularly when you'll be interviewing several candidates.
+ Maintain consistent questioning, typically following your organization's preferred questioning structure (your HR/Talent Acquisition partner should be able to help you with this). This allows you to compare candidates on similar questions/topics, giving a consistent, side-by-side comparison.

- Additionally, prepare questions that are specific to the job priorities or specialty areas; use these targeted questions to encourage the candidate to expand on his/her unique experiences that may bring desired qualifications to the position.
- Meet with employees in the role or a similar role to the one you're filling, to ensure that you're aware of projects, pain points, necessary skills and other attributes that are important. Connecting with those closest to the job duties will help you answer any questions the candidate may ask.
- If there are other people (a team leader, senior team member, your boss, etc.) whose perspective would be valuable, consider including them in the interview process.

Not only does preparation put you at ease as the interviewer, allowing you to engage in productive questioning and discussion with the candidate, it also puts the candidate at ease. Knowing that their experience has already been considered by the time they're sitting in the interview "hot seat" helps them to begin to form a connection to the organization, as well as to you, their potential new manager.

During the Interview

> "Hiring is a two-way street—the candidate is interviewing the manager, too! Be transparent about the company, culture, role, expectations, duties and other requirements!" -Michelle Baker

According to the Harvard Business Essentials book, *Hiring and Keeping the Best People* (2002), there are recommended guidelines for how your interview time should be spent:

Phase of the interview	What this should include	How much time should be spent
Opening of Interview	• Brief introductions of candidate and interviewer(s) • Setting expectations for how the interview will progress • Putting the candidate at ease	10% of interview time
Information Gathering	• Questioning the candidate about experience and qualifications • Discussion of organization, role and job responsibilities • Answering the candidate's questions	80% of interview time
Wrap Up	• Summarizing the discussion • Outlining next steps in the interview process • Answering any final questions • Thanking the candidate for applying and participating in the interview	10% of interview time

Your Role as the Interviewer

There are several interviewing techniques that companies utilize in the hiring process. Your HR/Talent Acquisition partner may provide you with an interview guide with recommended questions or a specific outline to follow, or at least share some recommendations and advice with you, especially if conducting an interview is new to you or something you do infrequently.

Your primary role is like that of a detective—after reviewing your "evidence" (job application, resume, notes from the initial phone screen), you're able to dig deeper and discover more about their qualifications, skills, and experience. At the same time, you're a representative of your organization and, more specifically, your team. Don't forget, the candidate is interviewing YOU as well!

Types of Interview Questions

Whether a first round or follow-up interview, there are several questioning methods that encourage a candidate to open up and share important details about their experience. In addition to scenario-based questions ("Tell me about a time when you demonstrated _____ skill.") or behavioral questions ("How would you respond in _____ situation?"), there is a simple method for balancing open-ended and closed-ended questions to gather deeper information from a candidate.

This method resembles an accordion—yes, the screechy, old-fashioned instrument:

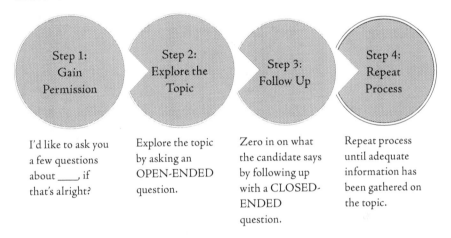

Step 1: Gain Permission	Step 2: Explore the Topic	Step 3: Follow Up	Step 4: Repeat Process
I'd like to ask you a few questions about ____, if that's alright?	Explore the topic by asking an OPEN-ENDED question.	Zero in on what the candidate says by following up with a CLOSED-ENDED question.	Repeat process until adequate information has been gathered on the topic.

Simply put: Ask better questions, get better information. Gather information that will help you discover a candidate's skills and qualifications to make an educated hiring decision.

Questions to Avoid

There are several questions that are prohibited during a job interview. Please refer to the Legal Appendix at the end of this book for helpful resources and consult with your Legal and Human Resources teams for your organization's specific guidelines.

After the Interview

Immediately after an interview, set aside some time to review and summarize your notes—it's recommended to do this before comparing notes with any other team members who participated in the interview. Doing this immediately following the interview will ensure that your discussion is fresh in your mind—it's easy to confuse answers among multiple candidates, particularly when asking similar questions.

The Society for Human Resource Management (SHRM) has developed a template for capturing a fair evaluation of a candidate. The Interview Evaluation Form below will help you, as a hiring manager, summarize your notes and provide a simple tool for side-by-side comparison of multiple candidates:

Interview Evaluation Form

Candidate Name _____ Job Role _____

Interviewer _____ Interview Date _____

Scoring Guidelines:

5 – Exceptional   4 – Above Average   3 – Average/Satisfactory   2 – Below
Average   1 - Unsatisfactory

Educational Background – Is the candidate's educational background or formal training appropriate or sufficient for this role?

(Circle One)   1   2   3   4   5

Notes/Comments:

Work History and Experience – Has the candidate developed skills through his/her work history and on-the-job experience that will be relevant for this role?

(Circle One)   1   2   3   4   5

Notes/Comments:

Technical Expertise – Does the candidate possess the technical skills necessary for this role?

(Circle One)   1   2   3   4   5

Notes/Comments:

Communication and Interpersonal Skills – Did the candidate utilize effective communication and interpersonal skills during the interview?

(Circle One)   1   2   3   4   5

Notes/Comments:

Passion and Enthusiasm – Did the candidate demonstrate interest in your organization, team/culture, and the role?

(Circle One)   1   2   3   4   5

Notes/Comments:

Knowledge, Research and Initiative – Did the candidate have a solid understanding of the organization, industry and role by doing his/her own research in advance? Was s/he prepared?

(Circle One)   1   2   3   4   5

Notes/Comments:

Core Values – Would this candidate embrace your organization's core values and mission?

(Circle One)   1   2   3   4   5

Notes/Comments:

Team/Culture Fit – Would this candidate be a good cultural fit for your team or organization?

(Circle One)   1   2   3   4   5

Notes/Comments:

Overall Impression – What is your overall impression of this candidate?

(Circle One)   1   2   3   4   5

Notes/Comments:

Recommendation – Would you recommend proceeding with this candidate to the next step of the interview/hiring process?

(Circle One)   1   2   3   4   5

Notes/Comments:

Making the Interview Personal

With a seemingly revolving door of candidates participating in the interview process, it can be challenging to make each interview feel personal for the candidate. As mentioned before, candidates are conducting their own interviews while being interviewed by you. In a job market where companies are fighting to hire and retain top talent, an outstanding candidate who knows his/her worth will be extremely cautious before committing to a new organization. It's a risky transition for professionals of all ages and experience levels.

Be transparent during your interview—celebrate what makes your organization and team special. Tell the candidate why you chose to work at the company—and more importantly, why you STAY. Give examples of how employees model the organization's vision, mission, and core values. Important to professionals of all generations, but particularly for Millennials, employees want to work with a purpose and a passion. They want to work for an organization they can believe in and that aligns with their personal values. While personal values are unique from candidate to candidate, being warm and enthusiastic about the company will invite candidates to imagine themselves as a part of your team and organization.

Just like in sales, a job interview requires a similar mindset to achieve a mutually beneficial hiring outcome. A successful sales professional will learn what's important to a customer before making an offer to sell. Once learning about the customer's priorities, the salesperson will highlight features and benefits that are relevant and meaningful to that customer.

Recently, a candidate interviewed for a faculty position with a university. The salary range was much lower than what the person was currently earning. The interviewer acknowledged the person's concern, but countered with, "You may earn less, but your children could attend here tuition-free!" That may have been an attractive benefit for some candidates, but this person has no children—therefore, it made no difference.

The lesson here? Take a moment to listen and learn what's important to each candidate you interview. Make your role in the hiring process relational, not transactional.

Tips for a Successful Interview

Here are a few simple tips for making the most of the job interview process:

- **Do your homework.** As you interview, look for candidates with skills, experiences, and a personality that will complement the rest of your team.
- **Take your time.** Schedule plenty of time—at least 45 minutes—with every candidate. Refrain from skipping questions because you "have a good (or bad) feeling" about someone. To effectively compare each candidate, you should spend ample time with each of them.
- **Look for patterns.** What does the candidate's work history tell you? Do they job-hop every couple of years? Do they change positions often? Do they place blame or provide excuses when asked about exiting a position or company, or when a project failed? Keep an eye out for red flags that may suggest performance issues.
- **Take note of body language.** Sure, it's normal for a candidate to be nervous during a job interview. But deliberate avoidance of eye contact, slouching, sweating, or other nonverbal cues that go beyond typical interview jitters may indicate a deeper issue—possibly a lack of confidence or an inability to back up their resume

or application. Depending on the role for which you're interviewing, consider whether these are traits you want representing your team, organization, and brand.

+ **Resist the urge to talk about yourself too much.** Sure, candidates are sizing you up during an interview, too. They're naturally curious about their potential new boss! Introductions and a brief explanation of your role aside, you're there to interview the candidate—not the other way around. You should be listening much more than you're talking.

+ **Don't be desperate.** Make it a priority to find the right person for the job. Don't settle for a "warm body" to simply fill a seat when you're short-staffed. In the long run, the investment in the hiring, onboarding, and training of the wrong person will cause much more stress on the morale and workload of your team. Communicate with your HR/Talent Acquisition partner that you won't compromise on finding a talented candidate that will fit the role, team, and organizational culture.

What happens if you skip this?

Failure to take charge during the interviewing and hiring process only puts unnecessary stress on yourself, the new employee you eventually hire, the existing team, and the organization itself, potentially:

+ Time and money wasted on inefficient recruiting and interviewing
+ Potentially choosing the wrong candidate for a role
+ Lowered team productivity, performance, and morale
+ Unsatisfactory customer service and satisfaction

The bottom line: Take the time to take ownership and accountability for each hiring decision you make.

Lessons Learned

Just like when you're planning a trip, you must map your starting point. The preparation that goes into navigating the employee development journey will ensure that you chart a course that sets an employee up for long-term success, beginning even before that employee joins your organization.

In this chapter, you discovered these key points:

- Starting with a well-crafted job description helps set clear expectations for candidates and employees.
- Determining Key Accountabilities and Job Benchmarks will identify skill gaps and narrow down the best candidate for the role.
- Investing time and effort into the interview and hiring process, as well as having a relentless commitment to finding the right candidate for the job—not just a candidate that "looks good on paper."
- Making the interview process relational, not transactional—candidates are choosing YOU just as much as you're choosing THEM.

Make it Happen

Follow these action steps to incorporate these key points with your existing and future team members:

- ✓ Do an audit of the job descriptions in your department. Are they accurate and up-to-date? What are the key accountabilities for each role?
- ✓ Meet regularly with your HR/Talent Acquisition partners to establish open communication regarding the recruiting, interviewing, and hiring process, as well as to discuss your staffing forecasts and potential hiring needs. Don't wait for an immediate staffing need to contact these helpful partners!
- ✓ If your HR/Talent Acquisition partner has an interview guide or resources to use, become familiar with them. If not, develop consistent interview questions to use in face-to-face, panel, and final interview scenarios.

Chapter 3

Onboarding: Crafting Your New Employee's Experience

"The success, engagement and loyalty of your new employee begins with the hiring manager, and the amount of effort put into his or her onboarding experience." - Michelle Baker

Navigating People

Companies are born from an idea. Someone has an ah-ha moment and says, "Wouldn't it be cool if we could…." And a company is born. Throughout my career, I've learned a great deal about how different types of companies view workplace learning and employee development. The sad truth is, it's often an afterthought. Somewhere between that initial cool idea and "Oh my goodness, we have 100 employees—maybe we should be DOING something with them," someone hopefully realizes that learning and developing new employees, as well as current and future leaders, should be a priority.

Recently, I had a conversation with an industry colleague who had been implementing an onboarding program for new employees at her company, a tech startup. It's a terrific process—one that involves a variety of stakeholders, that's been championed by the CEO, that welcomes new employees to the company, connects them to the team, and enables them to perform in their new roles. And unfortunately, it's a process that many of their hiring managers claim to be "too busy" to adopt.

Managers, everyone is busy. But the truth is, you're too busy NOT to provide a sufficient onboarding experience for your new employees. Furthermore, this is the price of admission for a manager—a key distinction between an individual contributor and a manager. Coaching and guiding both new and experienced employees is an important part of your job, even if there isn't a designated bullet point on your job description that says so.

Chapter Goals

In this chapter, you'll learn about the hiring manager's role in the onboarding process:

- Providing a welcoming, nurturing environment for your new employee
- Setting goals for the first weeks and months on the job
- Exploring career development opportunities early on

Whether this is your first time hiring a new employee, or if you're often bringing on new team members, you might find yourself lacking a consistent preparation process. The onboarding process doesn't start on the employee's first day; rather, it starts quite a bit earlier.

Bringing Life to the "Dead Zone"

Congratulations! After long interviews and countless meetings with your HR partners, you made an offer to a talented, dynamic candidate. Their background check was spotless and they've accepted the offer. Finally, a light at the end of the tunnel. That lonely, empty workstation in your department will soon have a new resident—but until then, the waiting begins.

If the candidate is currently employed elsewhere, it's likely that s/he will request time to put in a respectful two-week notice before starting with your organization. While you're eager to get your new rock star on the team, this is typical. After all, if an employee were to leave your team, you would hope for the same courtesy before leaving, right?

Even though you're in a bit of a lull, it's possible to connect with your incumbent, build rapport, and even set him on a path to learning—before day one.

This "dead zone"—that quiet period between an offer's acceptance and the new employee's start-date is a time where your new employee is ripe with a high natural level of engagement. He's likely wrapping up duties with his former employer and mentally "checking out." He's excited about the new opportunity on the horizon with your organization—and with you, his new manager. Take advantage of this engagement!

Your HR/Talent Acquisition partner should be communicating pertinent information with the new employee—standard paperwork (much of which is completed online now in many organizations), start-date/orientation details, and other logistics. The preboarding responsibility, however, doesn't fall on HR's shoulders alone. As the manager, you have an opportunity to begin creating a welcoming environment for your new team member.

Below are two to-dos lists to complete as you prepare for your new employee:

Preparing for the new employee's arrival	Welcoming a new employee to your team
✓ Make arrangements for computer/ technical equipment, phone, email and system access to be allocated ✓ Ensure that a furnished workstation, cubicle or office is available in your department/work area ✓ Order essential office supplies, if not readily available ✓ Order business cards, if needed ✓ If needed, arrange for company car, corporate credit card or other travel/ expense items ✓ Schedule Orientation and necessary training ✓ Schedule informal meet-and-greet meetings with key stakeholders across the organization ✓ Work with HR/Talent Acquisition partner for travel and relocation assistance, if needed ✓ Map out an itinerary for the new employee's first days/weeks on the job, including regular 1:1 time with you, his manager *What specific tasks must be completed at your organization to prepare for a new employee?* ✓ _____ ✓ _____ ✓ _____ ✓ _____ ✓ _____	✓ Announce to existing team members and key stakeholders about the new employee's arrival. ✓ Clean the workstation/cubicle/ office clean, and stock with essential supplies – post a welcome banner signed by the team. ✓ Send an "All About You" questionnaire to the new employee to learn about his/her favorite things (**see Appendix for template?**) – use that information to create a fun welcome kit to be waiting on the first day! ✓ If schedules/location permits, consider setting up a coffee or lunch meeting with the new employee to begin discussing the position, building rapport and calming nerves. ✓ Provide non-proprietary learning resources so the new employee can begin exploring your organization and/or industry on his own, easing the learning curve. ✓ Encourage existing team members and other organizational stakeholders to connect with the new employee on LinkedIn. ✓ Share the Twitter handles of must-follow company and industry leaders, so the new employee can follow and learn. ✓ Send a "swag kit" with branded promotional items to the new employee's home. ✓ Have the team create a team selfie or short homemade video with introductions to express their excitement for the new employee's arrival!

Simplify the Process

Orientation vs. Onboarding

Your new employee is starting on Monday morning. How much time have you, the manager, invested in planning his onboarding experience?

Chances are, HR is involved in planning for your new employee's arrival, along with the arrival of other new employees who are also starting that day. They may be coordinating the New Employee Orientation process, where, hopefully, they'll be receiving a solid introduction to your company, as well as general information that will help him become integrated with the organization.

But what about learning about his new team and role? Chances are, the Orientation experience is nearly identical for most new employees. As the hiring manager, you must be involved to ensure the onboarding experience is unique and relevant.

Orientation is an **event**. A rite of passage. It's a pre-determined period, typically spent dispensing basic information to employees as they begin with an organization. Time cards, payroll, benefits, security/compliance/regulatory training, building tours, and other essentials are common topics covered during this event. Many times, much of the basic content of this event will be led by your HR, Talent Acquisition, or Training partners.

Onboarding, however, is a **process**. Depending on the role or organization, the onboarding process can take anywhere from approximately 30 days to a year or more. It's not a one-size-fits-all experience. Because of this, the hiring manager is a crucial component to onboarding success. You're the link that will help the new employee build relationships. You're the mentor that will guide the new employee, answer questions, and set expectations.

There may be others on your team who are tasked with "training" a new employee, but that doesn't replace the critical need for building a solid relationship with you as the hiring manager and immediate supervisor.

During the employee's first days on the job, you should be meeting daily (sometimes multiple times per day) with your new employee. This is time spent processing what's being learned, and:

- Setting clear expectations about the job—schedule and working hours, policies and guidelines, communication preferences, and ensuring the new employee has the necessary tools and supplies available to do the job
- Discussing current and upcoming projects the employee will be involved with or leading
- Explaining how the employee's—and the department's—role fits into the big picture of the organization, and how the employee will interact with others
- Making introductions to others and helping your new employee form alliances up, down, across and outside the organization
- Helping your employee set performance goals for the first 30, 60, and 90 days—do the goals align with the job description? Do the goals align with the department and organizational priorities or strategic plan?

Again, your HR partner, departmental trainer, and other stakeholders certainly play an important role in the welcoming and engagement of a new employee during the busy first days and weeks. But those partnerships aren't a replacement for a new employee's meaningful relationship with a supportive hiring manager. The ultimate success, engagement, and loyalty of your new employee begin with you. The amount of effort you put into the onboarding process is a factor in that success.

Think you're too busy for onboarding?

The crux of a new employee's arrival is that your team has likely been operating on a leaner staff in the weeks (possibly months) leading up to his arrival. There's an inevitable pinch on time and resources for everyone involved, including you, the team leader.

Yes, everyone is busy. Having a lengthy onboarding checklist, daily one-on-one meetings, and other schedule-filling events can put a strain on you. You may be tempted to throw up your hands and say, "I'm too busy!"

Hiring manager, you're too busy NOT to provide a thorough onboarding experience for your newest team member. According to research from BambooHR, 31% respondents had left a job within six months of starting it. This tells us that new employees aren't always fully committed as they're getting started in their role at your organization. They may still be looking at job posting emails or checking up on applications submitted to other companies, in case a better offer comes along. The costs that go into replacing a lost employee go far beyond the price of simply recruiting and hiring a replacement; the morale of your existing team suffers greatly as the workload once again shifts unexpectedly.

The same research from BambooHR found that 33% of new employees said they wanted their manager or direct supervisor to be the one to show them the ropes. While several other stakeholders should certainly be involved in the onboarding process, the relationship with you, the hiring manager—even when you're busy—is the most critical to your new employee's success and retention.

Providing a Warm Welcome

Starting a new job is a process full of mixed emotions. The new employee is likely feeling excited, skeptical, motivated, and probably a dozen other feelings as Day One approaches. As a manager, your job is to ensure that feeling welcome and comfortable is among those emotions.

Try these simple strategies to make your new employee feel at home during the first days on the job:

1. Catch up with your new employee prior to the first day. If possible, meet in person; if that's not possible, make time for a phone call. Calm her nerves, answer her questions, begin talking about plans for her first week. Just knowing that plans are in place will ease the

jitters somewhat and instill confidence in your organization and in your leadership.

2. Assign a peer as a "buddy" within your department to work alongside your new employee during the first few weeks. This should be an experienced employee who models your organization's core values and understands the importance of being a go-to resource for information.

3. Leverage the new employee's prior experience by finding a way for her to contribute early on. Work together with your new employee to set actionable goals for the first 30, 60, or 90 days on the job so she can immediately feel like a productive member of the team.

4. Have a small treat, branded swag, fresh flowers, or a signed card from the team waiting on her desk when she arrives on her first day. Don't overlook the power of the seemingly tiny details—the small, welcoming gestures sometimes mean the most.

5. Take time to personally walk her around the office and introduce her to key individuals. Highlight her expertise in your introductions— show off your talented new team member and let others know how excited you are to have her on board!

6. Schedule a team lunch or social event sometime during the first week so she can become acquainted with the rest of your team.

7. Set aside a few minutes at the beginning and end of each day during the first couple of weeks to review daily plans, check in on early goals, answer questions, and debrief what the new employee is learning, observing, and doing.

Onboarding Goals

What are you hoping to achieve through onboarding your new employee? Obviously, you're adding a new person to your team and enabling them to perform their job duties. Onboarding goals should go beyond the basics. Since every new employee brings unique perspectives and experiences to your organization, onboarding can't be a one-size-fits-all process. Sure, checklists and templates may help expedite or prevent you from forgetting something important, but goals that are set should be specific to the employee and to the role.

30-60-90 Day Onboarding Plans

"Sink or swim" just doesn't work. Neither does the "drinking from the firehose" approach. New employees, even seasoned industry veterans, are still new employees. They still need to learn about your organization, products and services, team, and their personal role. This takes time. Remember, while orientation is an event—an important one, but an event nonetheless—onboarding is a process that takes several weeks or months. A process that you, the manager, must plan with intention.

Organizations have differing ideas about how long onboarding should take. Depending on the size and complexity of systems, procedures, products, and services, it could take up to a year for a new employee to truly be proficient in his or her role. Other, task-specific roles could yield a shorter time to productivity. It's important to determine what your new employee needs to learn to successfully perform his job duties, keeping in mind that most organizations need the onboarding process to be as efficient as possible. Also, even though employees are still learning over time, most don't appreciate being referred to as a "new employee" for long. Goal-setting should be carefully aligned with the employee's role and development needs—your new employee should never simply be assigned mindless "busy work" that yields no value or learning experience. When setting onboarding goals for your new employee, follow this onboarding-specific variation of the tried-and-true S.M.A.R.T. goal structure (see Appendix D):

Goal:	
Is this an immediate, short or long term goal? Anticipated completion date:	
What are the SPECIFIC elements of this goal that align with your new employee's learning needs?	

How will progress or success be MEASURED?	
What are the ACTION steps your new employee must take to achieve this goal?	
How is this goal RELEVANT to your new employee's role?	
How will this be TIME-BOUND? When and how often will you check in with your new employee?	

Key:

Immediate goals = realistic for first 30 days on the job
Short-term goals = realistic for the first 31-60 days on the job
Long-term goals = realistic for the first 61+ days on the job

Having specific goals allows your new employee to be immediately productive, utilizing the skills being learned on the job, as well as leveraging their expertise—usually one of the main reasons the new employee was hired in the first place. Having goals documented in writing also provides a "checks-and-balances" approach for monitoring your new employee's progress through ongoing discussion.

Career Development Begins Immediately

Many managers fall prey to the notion that new employees are "different" than veteran employees, and they're not ready to have discussions about career goals and development until they reach a certain milestone—at their first annual performance review, perhaps. Postponing career development discussions only sets limits: for your team's performance, for the organization, for your new employee himself. Making the connection between onboarding and long-term career development encourages your new employee to envision his long-term potential with your organization. If career growth and development is a key component of building employee engagement and retention, why not establish that from the beginning?

As you read in the previous chapter, there are tools to help you identify Key Accountabilities and Job Benchmarks. These can be used to help you onboard employees, assess job performance, and map out long-term career goals. As new employees join your team, utilize these tools to initiate productive discussion with them, as well as with your tenured teammates. To get started, templates and examples can be found in the Appendices.

What happens if you skip this?

The old saying goes, "People don't quit jobs; they quit managers." Many managers are unaware of their impact on a new employee's experience. Failing to establish a solid connection puts your talented new employees at risk of missing out on:

- Building rapport with others on the team, as well as with you
- Immersive learning experiences that deepen the employee's connection to the organization, team, products, services, and customers
- Deeper, open lines of communication

Bottom line: Onboarding breeds learning and loyalty. Recognize your role in that as the hiring manager.

Lessons Learned

Just like when you're planning a trip, you must map your starting point. The preparation that goes into navigating the employee development journey will ensure that you chart a course that sets an employee up for long-term success, beginning even before that employee joins your team.

In this chapter, you discovered these key points:

Learning and relationship building can happen during the period between offer acceptance and your new employee's start date—take advantage of their excitement and natural engagement!

As a manager, your connection and relationship with new employees is essential to their engagement, retention, and success.

Even the busiest managers are too busy NOT to provide a thorough, welcoming onboarding experience for a new employee. You must make onboarding a priority!

You should be initiating regular career development conversations with new employees from the beginning.

Make it Happen

Follow these action steps to incorporate these key points with your existing and future team members:

- ✓ Create a pre-boarding checklist to help you prepare for a new employee's arrival, including intentional opportunities to connect, to help put the new employee at ease, and establish a relationship prior to day one.
- ✓ Develop an onboarding checklist for your new employee's first week that includes orientation and other HR-led events, training opportunities, relationship building, on-the-job learning, and some down time to reflect and process. Include daily check-in time with yourself as well.
- ✓ Create a development plan to set onboarding and performance goals for your new employee's first 30, 60, and 90 days. Maximize his or her prior experience and celebrate quick wins!

Chapter 4

Career Maps: The Cornerstones are Key Accountabilities, Self-Awareness, and Re-calculating

"Everyone has talent. We all have the right to have our own path." - Lou Russell

Navigating Careers

As manager, the journey of someone else's career can seem confusing and hard to define. Think about where you are and how you got there, and you'll see that career paths tend to be crooked and accidental. Your job as manager is to coach, not to direct. Each person is unique and will have interest in their career, changing over time. No one can guarantee their future, but laying out a Career Map primes the pump and changes the way everyone sees opportunities.

Here's an example from one of my friends. Tom can trace his love for IT and being a "fixer" all the way back to his high school days. He'll tell you he was just getting by, not an overachiever, but also not one to have to try too hard. His senior year, he took the suggestion from a mentor to participate in a software programming class. The seed was planted, but he wasn't sold on making a career of it. He headed to college planning to earn a degree in business administration and accounting. His roommate was in the computer science program which led to many late nights of coding for them both. The passion became so strong, he dropped out of college and starting working as a programmer at a call center.

Over the course of the next several years, Tom found himself in several different jobs—IT help desk, tech for a retail technology store, manufacturing, and even politics until he came full circle back to IT. After working as the primary IT person in an organization, he realized he could do this on his own. His own company would fulfill his passion to problem-solve and help people. So, Tom did just that.

Today he's the founder and CEO of a successful IT organization. Once he put his dream out into the universe and was intentional about making it happen, he could see and achieve it. To him, that means he's able to live by his own rules, have the flexibility and capability to have a balanced lifestyle and provide for his family in a way that fills his passion. And, he says, "I can wear jeans everyday."

It may be that you are or will become the manager of a Tom. It doesn't matter whether your Tom is going to be there forever. You can help him (or her) navigate to the career that's best while doing impactful work today.

Goals of the Chapter

In this chapter, you'll learn how to build a Career Map, including:

- Defining your personal mission/purpose statement
- Using the mission to identify roles that fulfill that vision
- Creating key accountabilities that map from your current aptitude to your desired future
- Using self-awareness and self-regulation to adapt your personal Career Map by annually re-visiting your personal mission statement

A Career Map is an outline of different paths to move through a career and get to the job that fits your strengths. You've likely heard of a Career Plan, but notice a Career Map process is slightly different. Just like a real map, your Career Map will contain alternate routes, not just one specific path to one specific destination. This is a priority in the Talent GPS approach—like each person, each path is unique and not all employees should be expected to get to the same place.

Let Your Heart Sing

Your HR representative or supervisor may have helped you create a Career Plan at some point. As manager, help your team members take the time to think about what they each want. Communicate to them that their paths will and should evolve over a career. It may be the first time your staff member has been coached to work through a Career Map, especially one including alternatives.

In Appendix D Career Map, you'll find a template to use to coach your team members on how to build their own. To work through all the steps with an employee will take you at least four hours. Another option is to break this into four sessions, which are marked below, allowing the individual to have time to reflect and complete each before talking through the next.

Use these coaching suggestions as you work with everyone to think through the options:

1.   Start by thinking about all the activities, jobs, volunteer positions, and other activities that you've enjoyed. They may also want to include things they haven't experienced—for example, things they've "always wanted to try" or things they have no interest in. Brainstorm as many as possible.

Example of employee's response: Activities/ Jobs I've done or would like to do: server in a restaurant, intern at a TV station, intern designer for magazine, copy editor for student newspaper, instructional designer, learning facilitator, volunteer programming director of association, executive assistant, receptionist, event coordinator/ designer. I've always wondered what it would be like to be in sales, but I'd never want to be in accounting.

2.   Sort your list into two columns: things you'd like to repeat and things you you've decided aren't a good fit for you. Remember, these lists can change whenever you want, throughout your career.

Repeat	No Thanks
Magazine designer	Server
TV reporter / writer	Instructional design
Learning Facilitator	Receptionist
Programming Director	Executive Assistant
Event Coordinator / Designer	Accountant
Sales	IT Programmer

3. Group the things you like or you're excited to try. Check this list for themes. Review the list of activities you aren't thrilled about and determine if there were aspects of those roles you did like and if you want to add a theme for that.

Example of employee's response: The themes are creativity, flexibility, people facing, frequent change, influence, authority, helping others, visualizing and realizing a project from beginning to end, fast-pace

4. Leverage the results of any assessments you've used in the past. If you know your behavioral style, motivators/driving forces, and competencies (see Appendix B), compare them to the themes you've come up with. Prioritize these themes. Note to Manager: If you don't have access to these types of results, consider coaching your employee to ask others what they believe to be their strengths.

Example of employee's response: Example of strengths in DISC: as a High Dominance / Influencer, the themes of frequent change and influence are important. Driving Forces: Utilitarian / Individualistic, projects and authority seem important. Note to Manager: This may be a good place to stop and allow the employee to complete this reflection starting with Step 5 at another meeting.

Summary of Session 1:

Activities/Jobs	Repeat	No Thanks	What I loved	Things I didn't like
Server in restaurant		X	Fast pace People Flexible schedule	
Intern at a TV station	X		Meeting new people Telling a story Helping inform others	Being stuck in a newsroom Bad/ rough hours
Intern designer for a magazine	X		Creativity See a plan come to life	Rigid hours Working in cubes Too many constraints
Instructional Designer		X	Creativity Build a project from beginning to end	LOTS of constraints Too much structure Not always able to do what's best, but have to conform to what SME says
Learning Facilitator	X			
Volunteer programming director for local association	X		Meet new people Share new ideas Not a full-time position Leading a team/ committee	

Executive Assistant		X		Limited interaction with people Hours No influence Authority Creativity Processes & policies
Receptionist		X	Lots of people	
Event coordinator / designer	X		Work with people Visualize project from beginning to end Creativity Problem solving Fast paced	

Start Session 2:

Note to Manager: Reinforce that this process will lead to a Career Map that will likely have several different routes. There's no right or wrong answer and there's always opportunity for change. Continue to encourage responsibility—the employee has the authority to make those changes when necessary. To emphasize this, ask him or her to write the word DRAFT across the top of the template. The coaching continues:

1. Personal Vision & Mission: Now that the themes are clearer, you're ready to build a vision statement. This statement will describe what your life purpose is, or put another way, why you believe you were put on Earth. This is deep and may take a bit of time to complete. The finished statement is used to establish a base that you can return to as you make career decisions in the future. Like the themes, you can change this at any time.

    ◆ Think of as many verbs as possible that represent actions and describe things you love to do.

Sample: ignite, teach, build, advocate, facilitate, mold, foster, provide...

• Next make a list of nouns that describe what you value and the focus of your attention. You can also brainstorm whom it is you impact.

Sample: learning, growth, relationships, students, finances, Self, others, students, constituents, clients, neighbors, women, children ...

• The last step is to complete the puzzle. Pick three of the verbs from your list and one of the nouns and create a statement in this format:

I_____, _____, and_____ _____.

   (Verb)   (Verb)   (Verb)   (Noun)

Here's an example someone in the learning and development industry might use:

I *ignite, affirm,* and *sustain learning in self and others.*

You have permission to break a few rules here. Notice that there are three verbs:

ignite, affirm, sustain

One noun:

learning

And additional words to add more passion:

learning in self and others

Coach employees who are still trying to figure out what their dream job is to use this personal vision statement as they build their Career Map

(Appendix D) over time. For example, when a job that looks interesting comes up, encourage him or her to compare it to the personal vision statement. Does the job align? Does the team and culture align?

Note to Manager: Encourage your employee to play with this until it resonates with him or her. Recommend that the statement be short and to the point (less than 15 words) so that it's easy to remember and recite. Over time, you'll be able to share these, with your entire team contributing.

> Emotional Intelligence: Your direct reports who have reached the point in their career where they're doing exactly what they love, still find themselves frustrated by mundane, must-do aspects of their role. Encourage them to stop (emotional awareness) and recite his or her personal vision statement (emotional regulation) to get back to a more productive emotional place.

Bringing Home the Bacon

With a personal vision statement completed, it's time for you to help your direct report define the income they'd like to have. This number impacts their overall goals. For example, if it's important that you drive a fully loaded brand new car every two years, you'll need to find a role that comes with a substantial salary. On the opposite side of the spectrum, if it's more important to have tons of time off with a very flexible schedule, you may be open to less predictable income.

Refer again to the template to point out the matrix to brainstorm Have and Want:

Quadrant 1: Have / Want – the kind of lifestyle currently true and wanted.

Quadrant 2: Have / Don't Want – the kind of lifestyle elements that are currently true, but not wanted in the future.

Quadrant 3: Don't Have / Don't Want – the kind of lifestyle that's not currently true and not wanted in the future.

Quadrant 4: Don't Have / Want – the kind of lifestyle that's not currently true but wanted in the future.

Sample:

Have/Want:	Have / Don't Want:
Health	Credit card debt
Spouse	No degree yet
Don't Have/ Want:	**Don't Have / Don't Want:**
Financially stable including retirement	Trouble finding a job
Bachelors Degree	Trouble financing my children's college
Children	
Own House	

Using the brainstorming from the quadrants, create a list of actions and prioritize them using the criteria *"Want / Nice to Have / Need"*

Sample:

	Timing	Want / Nice / Need
Health benefits	Now	Need
Flexible Schedule	5 years	Nice

Start Session 3:

Mapping Your Path

Once you've built your base and determined what type of income is necessary it's time to start building a Career Map. As you begin to think about the steps that follow, continue to reflect on your personal preferences as well as your personal mission.

- Begin by building branches for the types of work you've decided to go after. Put an income range on each of these branches (check out job boards to validate the income in your area).
- Under each branch, list steps you'll take to get to the work and income you desire. If you want, put dates on the little branches—1, 5, and 10 years out.

- ✦ Put life events on the branches if it's relevant. For example, if you plan to have children, move, etc., consider how these play into your branches.
- ✦ Share with your boss. Revisit often and update as you continue to experience new roles and determine areas that do or don't work for you.

Here's a sketch:

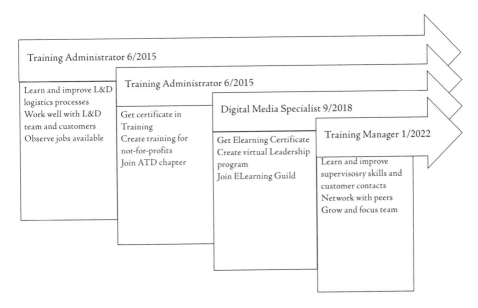

What happens if you skip this?

Without a plan, the uncertainty of each member of your team can build frustration and degrade engagement. Equally damaging to engagement is their expectation that you're in charge of their career. As manager, you can encourage and support the Career Map process. The time invested pays off in productive teamwork.

Lessons Learned

- Creating a personal vision as part of the Career Map will give your direct reports a solid base to return to throughout the different phases of their career.
- There's no right or wrong career plan to follow. Building a personalized Career Map with multiple paths creates a flexible process than can evolve.
- Career Maps are not a "one-size-fits-all" solution. Each team member's map will be different.

Make it Happen

- ✓ As a manager, you may be neglecting your career journey. Go through the steps above on your own career before working with your team.
- ✓ You may discover an employee who is going through the motions on a job, miserable because they have different goals. The goals may not map to those of your organization. Be authentic, and help them find the way to what makes their heart sing, even if it's only in the future right now.
- ✓ Remind your staff that a Career Map is a moment in time – it is their's to adjust and evolve.

Chapter 5

Promotion: Just Like Starting Over

> "A promotion is an opportunity to re-ignite purpose and passion that has been lost...and onboarding is fuel for the fire." - Michelle Baker

Navigating People

Once upon a time, there was an employee who was offered a promotion in another department. While the employee's current manager was supportive of the promotion, there was no immediate backup for the employee to assume her workload. The current manager met with the employee and the new manager to discuss a mutually beneficial transition plan. Unfortunately, a heavy workload meant the employee was required to wear two hats for several months until her old position could be backfilled. This resulted in a rushed onboarding plan, preventing the new employee from connecting with her new team, establishing herself as a leader, and learning the responsibilities of her new role. Ultimately, it significantly delayed her success and overall satisfaction, and she questioned her loyalty with the organization. Less than two years later, she accepted a position with another company.

Chapter Goals

Promoting an internal employee—whether elevating an existing team member to a supervisory role or bringing someone in from another department or division—is a process that requires careful planning and consideration. In many ways, it's like onboarding a new employee all over again, even when the employee has been with your organization for several years. As a manager, you're responsible for coordinating many aspects of the promotion process, which you'll explore in this chapter. These aspects include:

- Preparing for an employee's promotion
- Communicating with stakeholders about the promotion
- Creating a timeline and transitional onboarding plan
- Helping the promoted employee establish or evolve relationships with others

Preparing for an employee's promotion

When hiring for a position on the team, there are many things to consider as you interview and assess different candidates. Are you looking to hire externally, or would an internal candidate be a better fit for the role? Depending on the role, there are times when outside experience and perspective might be more appropriate. However, there are also times when promoting internally might be the best decision:

- When organization- or industry-specific skills are necessary to perform the job duties
- When the company culture is unique or challenging to fit in with
- When the department lacks documentation, processes, or training resources to support an external hire

And, of course, sometimes the best fit for the job is simply a person who's already employed by your organization.

As you prepare to promote an employee, setting expectations with your existing team members and others across the organizations is also necessary. When an employee has been with the company for a long time, s/he is "known" in a certain role or capacity, so changing the employee's focus in others' eyes will only help set the transitioning employee up for success.

Simplify the Process

Communicating with stakeholders about the promotion

Who needs to know about the employee's promotion? Once the proverbial cat is out of the bag, strategically managing the communication plan is always better than leaving it up to others to make assumptions (which, inevitably, will happen). Potential stakeholders might include:

- Existing team members, including those who the promoted employee might soon be supervising
- Team members in the promoted employee's exiting department
- Other department leaders, particularly in areas that frequently interact with your team
- Executives and other strategic organizational leaders
- Vendors, clients, and external contacts with whom the promoted employee will interact

When communicating to stakeholders, sending an uplifting, positive email is a good strategy to spread word of the promotion while at the same time building the promoted employee's credibility within the organization. Here's a sample communication that you can modify for your own needs:

FROM: John Smith
TO: Department Managers
SUBJECT: Organizational Announcement

All:

It is my pleasure to announce that Susan Jones has been promoted to Manager of Strategic Accounts on the sales team, reporting to me. Susan has been with ABC Company for 4 years in the role of Account Coordinator, where she was instrumental on key deals, including Superstore USA and Big Computers, Incorporated. Prior to joining ABC Company, Susan successfully led a sales team at XYZ Company, and brings a balance of practical experience and team leadership to this crucial role.

Susan will be transitioning into her new role over the next several weeks. During her transition, please direct needs to questions to me as she gets settled.

We are thrilled to have Susan leading our Strategic Accounts team – please join the sales team and offer your congratulations with some treats at a casual welcome reception for Susan next Friday, September 23, in the employee lounge from 3:00 – 5:00 p.m. We look forward to seeing you there!

Warm regards,

Communicating a promotion within the existing team

Sometimes, even when the promoted candidate is highly qualified and well liked, news of a promotion can be received with mixed emotions. Perhaps other existing team members interviewed for the position and were denied. Maybe the team has been tight-knit, and promoting an employee to a supervisory role will change the team dynamics. Possibly an "unknown" employee from another department is viewed as unqualified from the perspective of team members who have been performing the job duties for some time. Regardless of the reason, it's important for you to proactively communicate with your existing team:

- Explaining (not justifying) reasons why the promoted employee was selected

- Setting expectations for the transition and clarifying any changes to reporting structure
- Discussing logistics for the transition—timing, elements of the transition plan, who will be involved, etc.
- Requesting support from your existing team, and enlisting them to help secure a smooth transition

Existing team members possess a wealth of expertise that can benefit a promoted employee, particularly if the person is transferring from another department, division, or geographic location. Clarifying details of the transition will help squash some of the skepticism regarding the employee's qualifications for the role, and connecting them to the incoming employee will create an inclusive, welcoming environment, as well as increase the employee's chances for success in the new position.

What happens if the promoted employee has been a peer to others, working alongside them for months or even years? There are bound to be bumps in the transition, as workers figure out the team's "new normal," such as:

- A former peer becoming a supervisor, now having to address disciplinary or performance issues of those he used to be friends with
- An added "layer" of leadership—the current manager (possibly yourself), who may have been the team's direct supervisor, may now become a step removed in the departmental hierarchy, resulting in distance and unapproachability with the rest of the team
- Hurt feelings of those who feel they should have been selected for the promotion, or feel they are more qualified to do the job

Hosting a team meeting without the promoted employee in attendance to announce the promotion, discuss the transition, request assistance, and answer questions is an ideal strategy for communicating this to existing team members, allowing everyone to process the impending change. This is NOT a situation that warrants a blunt email. Scheduling this meeting at the end of the day is a good plan, so employees can leave for the day and process the announcement on their own terms. Following the meeting, however, make sure to check in with your team individually to see how they feel about the promotion and answer any questions that might have surfaced following the team meeting.

Creating a timeline and transition plan

Failure to plan for the promoted employee's transition affects everyone. Just like in the example at the beginning of this chapter, lack of planning eventually contributed to that employee's lack of satisfaction in her role, and ultimately with the organization. As you prepare for the employee to assume his/her new role after the promotion, consider these factors as you develop a timeline:

- Does the employee have to continue in his/her previous role for a period of time before fully assuming the new position? Will s/he be responsible for training a replacement?
- Is this a new or existing role within the team/organization? Is the promotion a backfill, or has a new position been created altogether?
- Does s/he need to relocate for the promotion?
- Is s/he taking on new, unfamiliar job duties for which specific training or certification is necessary?

In most cases with internal hiring and promotion, simply "flipping the switch" from the old to the new is not an option. Taking stock of logistics of the transition will help you, the employee's former manager, and certainly the promoted employee himself.

Most of the time, an employee will have the blessing of his/her existing manager before even pursuing a new position in another department, so news of a promotion is rarely a surprise to a manager. Once the decision has been made and the job offer has been accepted, set up some time to meet with the transitioning employee and his manager, to discuss current projects, job duties, and to craft a plan mutually beneficial for all impacted.

Onboarding, again

Once the transition timeline has been established, you're back in onboarding mode. The promoted employee may have a long tenure with the company, but there are inevitable gaps in skill, knowledge, and experience that will need to be addressed for the promotion to be a success. In fact, the perspective of the company might be totally different from this new vantage point, so in many ways, promotion is like starting all over. Together with your promoted employee, review the job description and discuss the key responsibilities of the role:

Skill/Knowledge/ or Experience to be Learned during transition	What resources are available to provide training, experience or support?	When should this be complete?
(example) Learn how to approve time sheets, conduct performance reviews and other supervisory duties	• Attend New Manager Orientation workshop, hosted by Learning & Development team • 1:1 coaching with manager to observe current performance review preparation/delivery process • Access job aids with instructions on how to approve time sheets, time off requests, etc	• Attend next offering of workshop (October) • Ongoing coaching with manager
(example) Meet key clients and vendors with whom the team interacts	• Manager sends introduction email to each client and vendor contact • Promoted employee joins next meeting/conference call with each client/vendor to make personal introductions • Promoted employee meets with each account coordinator for each client to discuss account history, health, challenges, etc • Promoted employee uses CRM system to research details	• Introduction emails sent before end of month • Client meetings attended within 30-60 days, as scheduled • Account coordinator meetings scheduled within 30 days • Self-paced CRM research – ongoing

As you can see, these basic examples don't necessarily include learning about the core elements of the organization. Rather, this point is to address the specific skills that must be mastered to successfully perform the new role. This can't be a cookie-cutter plan. Each candidate brings their own unique perspectives and experiences, and those will determine what needs to be learned. And, to make things even more complex, "training" isn't always the solution. The 70:20:10 learning model suggests that the most effective learning happens through informal, practical means. Let's break the model down:

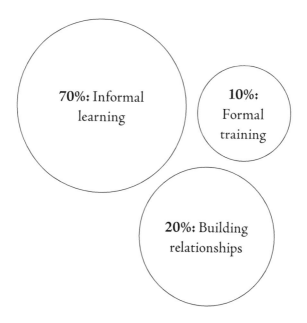

Think about when you first learned to ride a bike. The likelihood that you enrolled in a Bike-Riding 101 class is probably slim. Maybe you had someone instruct you on how the bike was put together, or they let you help them assemble and you learned a little bit of bike mechanics. Let's call that your 10% of "formal instruction." Now, you probably had someone—a parent, older sibling, maybe a neighbor—helping you out, coaching you, and holding you steady until you were ready to ride solo. Think of that as the 20%—relationships, coaching, and mentoring. But when did it finally catch on? When they let go, and you just started riding. Sure, you probably fell and scraped your knees a few times, but after some practice—the 70%—you mastered the skill and were off, flying around your neighborhood.

Workplace learning and transitioning into a new role aren't much different. There must be elements of formal training, relationship building, and practical, on-the-job experience to fill the gaps. An important process to follow, just as you would during the hiring process, is to identify Key Accountabilities and establish Job Benchmarks to identify the promoted employee's gaps. Then, as you consider your promoted employee's onboarding and transitional learning needs, consider these simple methods to incorporate a mindful blend of each facet of the 70:20:10 model into your promoted employee's onboarding and learning plan:

70% - Informal Learning	20% - Building Relationships	10% - Formal Training/ Instruction
• Job shadowing with teammates or other departments with whom the new employee will frequently interact • Observation of job duties being performed • Casual Q&A sessions or project debrief meetings • Stretch assignments • Cross-functional projects • Providing "just-in-time" job aids and self-paced resources (wikis, FAQs, documentation, videos, checklists, etc) • Conducting industry and competitor research as appropriate	• Regular coaching with direct supervisor • Connecting the promoted employee with a team "buddy" during the transition • Identifying a mentor for the promoted employee • Setting up casual "meet-and-greet" meetings with key individuals across the organization • Organizing a team lunch during the transition • Inviting the promoted employee to a "skip-level" lunch with his boss and boss' boss • Introductory meetings with clients, vendors and other external stakeholders • Connecting with others on LinkedIn or other social media platforms	• Company-specific training – systems, processes, procedures, products, professional development skills, etc • Manager training as appropriate • eLearning modules via your organization's Learning Management System (LMS) • Webinars and virtual training sessions • Assigned reading – industry books, whitepapers, research reports, etc • Certification programs • Formal leadership development programs • Industry conferences and seminars

Remember, templates, examples and other details for setting Key Accountabilities and Job Benchmarks and identifying gaps can be found in Appendix B.

It bears repeating that most tenured employees should have a solid idea about your organization's vision, mission and core values, so a promotion transition/onboarding plan can typically bypass the basic "company introduction" components that would be covered with a brand-new employee during Orientation. However, making a fresh connection to your organization is always a good idea! In a previous role, the line of sight to the organization's purpose may have been quite different. Helping your newly-promoted employee re-establish that line of sight in his/her new role will help ensure that the connection s/he felt to the company in the past will continue, and grow stronger, in this new season of employment.

Developing your new leader

It's possible that in this position, your promoted employee is embarking on his/her first leadership role. As the manager, you have an ideal perspective for guiding your promoted employee through the transition, helping him/her begin the leadership development journey. Questions to consider:

+ Does your organization offer leadership development programs and opportunities?
+ Is there an established leader outside your department who can serve as a mentor?
+ What resources can you provide to foster self-paced learning and discovery?

Remember the 70:20:10 learning model as you build a leadership development plan; this blended approach will immerse your newly promoted employee in the role and allow him/her to explore all facets of learning and leadership.

Relationships, old and new

Solid working partnerships are the linchpin to success for teams and organizations. Employee transitions, including promotions, undoubtedly impact team dynamics. Helping your promoted employee nurture and evolve existing relationships and forge new ones is a supportive hat you should wear as the manager. Consider the different challenges your new employee may be encountering during his/her transition:

- Former peers becoming the employee's new direct reports
- Joining a new department and meeting new employees
- Aligning work with other departments that the employee rarely worked with in the past
- New relationships with senior leaders and executives
- Meeting clients, vendors, and other external stakeholders
- A new dynamic between the promoted employee and yourself

Helping your promoted employee build alliances is a privilege as a manager. Regularly discuss the impact of relationships in your one-on-one meetings and coaching sessions. Personally extend introductions. Build up your promoted employee's credibility with these partners. Help him/her navigate unfamiliar, confusing office politics. In the end, you'll be increasing your employee's confidence and improving organizational relations, while continually building a solid relationship with your employee.

What happens if you skip this?

Promoting an employee is a unique opportunity to not only elevate a high-performing individual within the organization, but it also sends a clear message to employees across the organization that growth and internal career development are available to those who earn it. By not managing the promotion process, you disrupt harmony amongst the existing team and others with whom you interact:

- Relationships within the team suffer when communication isn't clear about why an employee was chosen for the promotion

- Relationships up, down, across, and outside the organization are compromised when the promotion isn't clearly communicated
- Not setting expectations on a transition plan affect the employee's former role, as well as delay their immersion and learning in their new role

Lessons Learned

Promoting an employee is an exciting leg of the employee development journey. As a manager, you get the opportunity to elevate an employee to a new level. Regardless of whether this is an employee who's been part of your team, or a high-performing individual from another part of the organization, you get a front-row seat as this person embraces a new opportunity, learns about new responsibilities, and realizes his/her potential.

In this chapter, you learned these key points about how to support your newly promoted employee and make the most of learning opportunities during the transition:

1. Setting expectations with existing team members and other important stakeholders is critical to prepare for the promoted employee's transition.
2. Creating a proactive communication plan to promote and celebrate your employee's promotion helps generate excitement and boosts the employee's credibility within the organization.
3. Promotion is like onboarding all over again—even when the employee has worked for your company for a long time.
4. The most effective learning happens through a deliberate blend of formal training, relationship building and informal, practical experiences (think 70:20:10).
5. Establishing new relationships and allowing existing relationships to evolve can be tricky, but it's a necessary part of the transition.

Make it happen

Follow these action steps to incorporate these key points into your promoted employee's transition plan:

- ✓ Meet with the promoted employee's current manager, if applicable, and create a transition plan and timeline that is mutually beneficial.
- ✓ Make a list of the potential stakeholders, internal and external, who will be impacted by the promotion.
- ✓ Consider your communication strategy for each of the stakeholder groups
- ✓ With the promoted employee, review the job description and list the skills and knowledge that will be needed in the new role.
- ✓ Create an onboarding and learning plan that incorporates a blend of formal training, relationship building and practical, on-the-job experience.
- ✓ Look for opportunities to make introductions and connect the promoted employee to individuals, teams and external parties with whom s/he will frequently interact.

Chapter 6

Succession Plan: Building Your Own Replacement Without Blowing Up Your Team

"There will always be turnover. Too much, and your company is unable to deliver. Too little, and your company is stagnant."- Lou Russell

Succession Planning is an often misunderstood and secretive non-process. My first job was as a programmer at the old AT&T, the epitome of bureaucracy. Like most young, new employees, I was determined to climb quickly in the organization. After all, I got good reviews and I did good work. I would read the weekly company newsletter, see someone I knew was promoted who, in my judgmental opinion, was not as strong as I was. My peers and I whined over coffee - "why did 'that jerk' get promoted?!" With a little experience, I realized that people would say the same about me when I did get promoted. We were set up in a competition that didn't drive teamwork or alignment.

I was sponsored by an executive friend to be part of a closed, quasi-secret group of high-potential employees. We had speakers and meetings, but no clear plan for what we were supposed to be learning or how to manage our career paths. I'm sure the people who weren't asked to participate were frustrated and demotivated by this process, and our supervisors were out of the loop as well. In this chapter, you'll learn how to reinforce as a manager these four important facts with your direct reports:

1. Promotions are not always fair (to you).
2. Promotions are not based JUST on good performance.

3. You won't get promoted if no one knows you want to be.

4. If you aren't ready when a promotion is available, someone else will be chosen.

Navigating Careers

We had the privilege to develop and lead a custom experiential leadership program for over 300 Leaders at Medco, which is now Express Scripts. Top performers were nominated by the executives to participate in this program. Each learner received coaching on their individual development plans during and for at least six months following the program. The leadership was serious about developing leaders.

Medco was a pharmacy benefit management company with IT and pharmacist leaders. It was a competitive culture. The company was created from a split with Merck. The executive leadership team knew that Medco had the potential to grow very quickly, and growing talent would be the key. Succession Planning had to be done differently. High-performing staff would have to be able to move up quickly and replace themselves quickly, without stopping the progress of the team. The executives coached their leaders to look at Succession Planning this way: if you want to move up, you have to build your own successor(s) to replace you. Each leader at every level had this succession goal as part of their performance review. For every leadership position, there was supposed to be a replacement ready to step in.

We saw a difference in this company compared to others we had worked with:

+ These leaders didn't see themselves as competing against each other for positions. Instead, they were competing to grow their teams quickly and effectively, ensuring future new opportunities. There was no secret plan—you got promoted if you got your team ready and you had the talent to push on. In a quickly growing business, there are plenty of opportunities.

- The leaders prioritized time to grow their replacement because it was in their best interest.
- The great leaders also communicated their plan to their whole team so it wasn't a secret game. Anyone could grow, but they had to do the work. Anyone could also stay where they were.

Now when I search LinkedIn, it's clear these leaders still have impressive careers. This approach drove engagement and personal responsibility well beyond their time at Medco. Equally impressive, all levels of leaders from the organization have thrived. As a manager, you have the power to grow both your own career and that of the future leaders of your organization in the same way.

Chapter Goals

In this chapter, you'll learn a process for Succession Planning which includes how to:

- Leverage the Key Accountabilities of a leader position
- Establish gaps between the leader position and the prospective candidates
- Prioritize the prospects and provide feedback to each
- Review the Career Maps for each prospect (see also Career Planning Chapter 4) to create a pool of candidates
- Revisit quarterly

Like each of the chapters in this book, Succession Planning is tightly connected to the entire Talent GPS process. As in other chapters, I'll recommend paper-based and assessment based approaches for the process which will be found in Appendix D as well.

Simplify the Process

Succession Planning is the process of strategically choosing the candidates who can best replace you when you move to another job. Before you can be promoted or transferred, your current role must have a competent new owner. Historically, this has been the responsibility of the leader. In Talent

GPS, we encourage you to manage your own Succession Plan and coach your staff on building theirs.

There are many challenges to building effective Succession Planning:

- Leaders are fearful of making a replacement list because it could make it easier to fire or bypass them. As leaders climb in a hierarchical organization, there are fewer opportunities for advancement. Take a deep look inside—is this true for you?

- Busy-ness is an easy excuse for not getting Succession Plans in place. Multi-tasking is epidemic. Busy is part of being a leader; it comes with the job. Being promoted will not lessen your busy-ness. It's important to figure out how to manage busy if you want to grow your career.

- Being explicit about succession is critical for supervisors. Your employees may not see the criteria for being promoted, so they guess. They confuse "kissing up" to influencing effectively. This is a cancer that drives distrust and competition in teams. One of these people can create havoc on a team.

- Leaders of leaders live in fear that at any moment a top performer on their team will jump for a better offer, leaving the organization in turmoil. As manager, you must prioritize the time to revisit your Succession Plan with your pool of candidates regularly. Succession Plans, tuned through regular communication, drive engagement.

- The jobs of the leader and manager are focused on very different things. As their leader, you must teach your candidates that if you want to be promoted, you'll have to be competent at politics. An effective leader is driven by and skilled at acquiring power, and s/he knows how to read the playing field of politics. Some of your staff may be very good at running projects, getting things done, and communicating well with stakeholders, but they don't understand the politics of influencing up. You must be clear with your direct reports that the next level requires you to change your approach—ironically, the very approach that has made you successful so far.

♦ No leader or team member can build a Succession Plan without collaborating well with others. If you have people reporting to you, you must be both a successor and develop successors concurrently.

Here are the important deliverables required for effective Succession Planning (see Appendix D Succession Plan). You may already be familiar with many of these deliverables when they were discussed in Hiring (Chapter 2), Onboarding (Chapter 3), and Career Map (Chapter 4).

♦ Key Accountabilities (see Appendix D Key Accountabilities): for a person's current role, 3-5 statements explaining what the specific job must deliver for the organization to thrive (candidate and leader)

♦ Job Benchmark (see Appendix B Job Benchmark): based on the Key Accountabilities, a prioritized list of behaviors, priorities

Here's an example of how a lack of Succession Plan can go horribly wrong. A highly respected C-level executive was hired to save a critical department. He accepted the role as a short-term gig. There were no Succession Plans. He reorganized the entire department by hiring and promoting talented young managers into leadership positions and changed the culture to focus on the priorities of the business. As he prepared to leave the short-term gig to retire, he realized that, although his team had lots of potential, they were still too new to their positions to provide the breadth of knowledge and experience required. His only choice was to find an outside replacement.

It was a policy at that time that C-level new hires were required to shadow the existing leader for a full year. The two worked carefully together, but having two leaders is confusing to a department. A headhunter came after the new executive with a big check and he was gone. It took another year to find a replacement. Had the business prioritized Succession Plans as a required process, there would have been a plan in place from the start.

Assume this organization has found a new leader. Assuming that work is still overwhelming and in transition, what three priorities should the new leader do to stabilize the Succession Plan for himself and for his direct reports as quickly as possible? What things should the direct reports be doing to help the new leader and to be prepared for promotion in the future if that's their goal?

(driving forces) and business acumen for the *current* specific job (candidate and leader)

- Gap Report (see Appendix D Gap Report): a report that compares the Job Benchmark for a job to a person to establish the strengths and opportunities for improvement (candidate)
- Career Map (see Appendix D Career Map): a project plan with measurable goals to grow the proficiency of a person to meet the needs of future job(s)
- Succession Plan (see Appendix D Succession Plan): by using all the resources above, the strategic process to prepare the best 3-5 candidates to replace you so you can be promoted

Note the difference and at the same time the connection between a Career Map and a Succession Plan. A Career Map is focused on your *self*-career future. A Succession Plan is focused on *others*—people who could replace you so that you can be promoted. As a leader, it's important to have both and encourage your team members to do the same. The leader who wants to be promoted is always working on growth opportunities for a higher position, just as each team member is doing so for the role they'd like to move into. All employees who want to climb higher in the organization, from any level, need to focus on improving their match with the job they are in while also preparing to match the next job.

Notice the relationships below and how these deliverables work together. The Key Accountabilities and Job Benchmark describe the specific JOB. The Gap Report is built by comparing the Job Benchmark (the JOB) to the PERSON using the person's unique Talent Report. Finally, a PERSON can leverage the results of a Gap Report to build a Career Map.

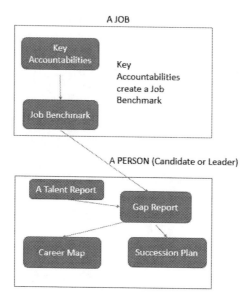

See Appendix D for templates or specific chapters for each of these steps.

The intersection of the JOB with the PERSON must be done very carefully. There are times when a person is in a job that doesn't match their strengths. It doesn't mean s/he is a bad employee—it means it's the wrong job for them. When managers abandon the base criteria for a job (Key Accountabilities, Job Benchmark) and shorten the process by picking people they like, this mismatch can easily occur. You may think that you can read candidates, but everyone has bias. By the same token, the employee may suspect that the match isn't great, but it's difficult to turn down a promotion with more income and status.

Clarifying the difference between the JOB and the PERSON also creates more compliance because your process is defendable. To stay compliant, it's critical that the same process be followed for all. Considering the JOB and PERSON requires not only diagnostic assessments, but also conversations and discussions between the leader, candidates, and references.

Below is a template for what you as the leader (with candidates) will do to facilitate Succession Planning. The steps of the process are:

+ Quantify/ update the Key Accountabilities of the leader position
+ Establish gaps between the leader position and the prospective candidates
+ Prioritize the prospects and provide feedback to each
+ Review the new Career Maps for each final candidate
+ Revisit at least quarterly

Quantify the Key Accountabilities of the leader position

For Succession Planning to work, the JOB and the PERSON must be established. Key Accountabilities create a measurable and actionable set of job requirements. Each employee should always have a current list of Key Accountabilities.

It's common for companies to promote from within but hire outside to bring in C-Level executives. Pretend you're a direct report of a retiring C-Level. How would you feel about this bias toward hiring from outside the company? How would it impact your career planning?

What could you do to change the bias and bring attention to your fit to the job? Looking at this Forbes list, which of these attributes of executive presence are best for you to showcase? What opportunities can you ask for to prepare for the CIO role?

http://bit.ly/2ot2goN

1. Excellent Public Speaking, Command a Room
2. Assertiveness (not Confrontational)
3. Emotional Intelligence
4. Sense of Humor
5. Good Posture, Open Body Language

Establish gaps between the leader position and the prospective candidates

POTENTIAL Candidate	Leader
ONGOING: Review the Key Accountabilities of your current role. Propose updates if they are out of date. This will likely require review with your boss and HR for final approval. Revisit your Gap Report created by comparing your strengths and opportunities to the Job Benchmark for your Job. Build or update a Career Map if you have not already done this.	ONGOING: Review the Key Accountabilities of your current role. Propose updates if they are out of date. This will likely require review with your boss and HR for final approval. Revisit your Gap Report created by comparing your strengths and opportunities to the Job Benchmark for your Job. Build or update a Career Map if you have not already done this
	INITIATE: Identify and invite a potential candidate pool. You will refine this pool in the later steps so you will select more than you will keep. Communicate carefully to each potential candidate how this process will work and the choice will be made. Allow them to opt out if they want. Clarify that each candidate must build their succession candidate pool to be considered for promotion.
Review the Key Accountabilities of your boss' role when you receive them. Carefully consider whether this is a job that you feel fits with your goals and your strengths.	Provide the Key Accountabilities of your current role to the potential candidates.
Compare the two different Key Accountabilities and identify differences and similarities. Begin to make notes on how you would bridge gaps that you may have with the potential new job.	Schedule and hold time to complete and review the Gap Reports (next step) for the potential candidates in advance.

Prepare to share your Succession Plans with the leader. Clarify specifically how quickly you could take the job and who would replace you.	Review the Succession Plans of each of the candidates. The strength or weakness of these plans will also be part of how you choose your final candidates.

Prioritize the prospects and provide feedback to each

POTENTIAL Candidate	Leader
Provide your current Talent Report (or build one) and compare that to the Leader's Job Benchmark to create a Gap Report for the Leader's role.	Review the Gap Reports against your job and each of the candidates. Share with the candidates to prepare for the review already scheduled. Prepare your choices by comparing the potential candidates to each other.
Discuss the results of your Gap Report with your leader 1-on-1. Be prepared to discuss the notes you made in the last step regarding the difference between your current job and the leader's job. Be well versed in the Gap Report and notice your strengths and opportunities for improvement.	Discuss the results of the Gap Reports with each of the potential candidates 1-on-1. It is likely that the results will be very similar, so you will ask clarifying questions about differences in strengths and opportunities.
Based on the discussion, update your Career Map and Succession Plan. Share with the Leader.	There will likely not be obvious choices but you'll know what you're getting and NOT getting from each candidate. The Gap Report will also provide you with information to encourage ongoing development on the candidates Career Map, for those who are not selected this time.

Review the new Career Maps for each final candidate (see also Career Planning chapter).

POTENTIAL Candidate	Leader
Receive the information from your leader about whether you will be a candidate at this time. Use the information, disappointing or exciting, to focus you attention on your current job and future role desired.	Determine the 3-5 candidates best currently to succeed you. After the candidates have accepted, share with the entire organization. Explain that this process may be repeated frequently.
Update your Career Map and Succession Plans based on what you have learned and share these with your leader.	Be clear and concise with those who were not chosen, explaining to them the reasons and ways they can move into this job in the future, or another if it is true.

Update and manage ongoing development

FINAL Candidate	Leader
Update the Career Map quarterly or when responsibilities in either current or future jobs change.	Assign relevant work and projects to final candidates to build capacity. Request the candidates add these to their Career Maps.
Observe your boss and continue to notice gaps between your current job and the next. Aspire to replicate your boss' best strengths and behaviors.	Continue to add / remove from the succession list as situations change, but strive to always have one or two top candidates ready.
Proactively ask for opportunities to grow experience and strength.	Share your succession choices with your peers and boss.
Communicate development requests and work quarterly to your leader.	Provide feedback regularly on all behaviors and choices of the candidates.

Since the world is changing, Succession Plans need to be revisited at least quarterly. To ensure seamless transition, always have the date of the next review of Career Plans when you complete the current review.

What happens if you skip this?

Leaders without Succession Plans are either unorganized or unsure of themselves. If you're a leader who's too busy for Succession Plans, you're too busy for a promotion. If you're a leader who fears that building a Succession Plan will provide your company with your replacement, you're not doing a good job and you know it.

A great leader knows that his or her primary role is to grow those who will lead in the future. This requires attention, intention, and humility. If your staff doesn't believe you hold their future in trust, they won't feel engaged in the business. Your turnover will increase and your outcomes will decline.

Lessons Learned:

Return to your Action Plan and consider the following take-aways:

- Do you and your direct reports have up-to-date Key Accountabilities used to build a Job Benchmark?
- Do you and your direct reports have a current Career Plan based on their current job? Have you discussed this plan with your direct reports in the last three months?
- Do you have a successor candidate pool of 1-3 candidates who can replace you if you get promoted? Is this documented in a Succession Plan?
- Have you ensured your direct reports have a Succession Plan as well?
- Have you identified jobs that you would like to have in your company? What's your strategy for ensuring that those who promote know that you're interested in these jobs?
- Do you know what jobs your direct reports would like to have?
- Do you know of candidates who are in other areas that you would like to have in your area? How can you work with a direct report to make this happen?

Make it Happen

- ✓ Change the mindsets of your peers and staff. Emphasize that the employee owns their succession, and the manager's job is to advise them without doing it for them.
- ✓ Not all employees will want to be promoted.
- ✓ As a manager, you play a parallel role with the staff who wish to be promoted. For them to be promoted, you must move to another job. While you are advising them, you will also be planning your next move.

Chapter 7

It's In Every One of Us - From Where They Are to Where They Can Go

"Talent means people. Each one of these people is unique and gifted."- Lou Russell

Like GPS, there's more than one path through a career. A new college graduate frantically seeks to lock down a successful career knowing very little about the real world of work. After a few years, this worker will realize that the path to the dream they made up in their heads when they left college was just that—a dream. Some will get discouraged and dream smaller. Some will be encouraged and dream bigger. All will enter a world completely different than what they expected. Leaders in a company can choose to play a significant role in helping each of their team members make the best choice at pivotal moments of their career. Peers can help as well. It's the core responsibility of a leader to hold in trust the people they lead and it's sacred work. Leaders must remember:

1. Promotions occur when a person and a job match. Job fit is more important than expertise, knowledge, history, and desire.
2. Career development occurs every day for leaders and teams. Each day is an opportunity to step up.
3. Both a leader and each team member share the responsibility for their own career and the careers of those they lead.
4. Honesty, feedback, and authenticity are the cornerstones of growing organizations through the growth of their people.

Navigating Careers

You may be in a situation where your company doesn't support career growth and planning. Lean on a peer group. Your shared goal will be to improve each other. Here are examples from my peer group of how we've helped each other implement Talent GPS:

- A family-owned national rehabilitation company negotiated an employee-ownership transition. A top employee clear about her strengths was offered the CEO position. She determined that her best match was the COO role. Her peer with different strengths became the CEO. Job matching drove company performance. Up isn't always the best path, and lateral moves may offer a better fit.

- A company lost its founder and CEO to illness. The loss was heart-wrenching and threatened to paralyze the tightly knit business. A silent and retired partner had re-entered the company to help during the illness, but he didn't want to keep working the number of hours required to lead the company. There were two other leaders with ownership. My peer explained to us that the decision to fill the president's role needed to be made quickly to keep customers and employees confident. As a group, we confronted him with, "Why couldn't you be president?" He reminded us that he needed to manage the Operations and Sales organizations for continuity. We confronted him again—"Why couldn't you do all three and develop your managers to do Operations and Sales?" He looked up and saw his future clearly as President. Your peers can be your best career allies.

- A large agricultural firm was the expected life-long career for one of our members. At all times, he could recite his future career path. He planned his next two or three career moves at the company and his leaders agreed. The path was straight but there were some surprises, and moves were made more quickly and in unexpected places as acquisitions and changes in the marketplace occurred. He never lost a laser focus on his career—where he could make an impact and how it would impact his family. During a recent acquisition, he was disappointed when the job he wanted was given as a political move to another. The role offered to him didn't match his plan and didn't meet his goals for impact and family. He took a new path, and recently negotiated a role as CEO and partial owner of a well-funded start-up. Keep your eyes and ears open because there are always other opportunities. Don't limit your dreams.

Take a moment and think about where your honest feedback can come from. It's invaluable. I've learned these lessons from my peers:

- These leaders don't see themselves as competing against anyone else for positions. They focus on what's best for the business, best for their team, and best for their families. Their priorities are always clear and focused.
- They are each clear about their own strengths and blind spots. They leverage others to fill in the holes. They know that as a whole, each team is greater than its parts.
- They build the leaders that will replace them intentionally and honestly. They provide regular feedback, positive and developmental. There are no secrets.
- Hiring and onboarding are critical, providing clear processes that ensure a solid team. Time is prioritized to invest in growing people because the staff is the glue that ensures a cohesive community.
- They map their careers and each of them can tell you at any time where they are and where they want to go. They expect the same of their teams.

Goals of This Chapter

In this chapter, you'll learn a process for transitioning to and implementing the Talent GPS process, which includes:

- Creating sponsorship and buy-in
- Defining the boundaries of the initiative
- Creating a communication strategy to sell the dream
- Helping everyone delegate effectively
- Asking: what does SUCCESS look like?

As in other chapters, there will be paper-based and online tools for the rolling out of the entire Talent GPS process. All tools can be found in the Appendix that follows.

You can't build what you can't see. Using the brainstorming that you've done in this Sidebar, begin to create measurable tasks to implement and transition to the Talent GPS process for your team, organization, or company. While the Talent GPS will be an ongoing, repeatable process, transitioning to the Talent GPS process is a project. You'll learn how to work out the specifics of the project in this chapter.

Simplify the Process

Here are important questions to answer before transitioning to the Talent GPS process:

> + You're busy. How will you find the time to implement and sustain these processes?
> + Everyone else is busy. How are you going to sell the Talent GPS process and maintain momentum with your team, peers, and leadership?
> + This may be a scary change for your team, peers, and

leadership. There will certainly be some people that would rather leave it the way it is now. Who are they and what will help get them on board?

Measuring Talent GPS Success

Imagine that you'll go to sleep tonight and when you wake up tomorrow morning, a miracle has occurred. You return to work to find that the entire Talent GPS process has not only been implemented but also completely accepted by the entire company. Describe what you see:

HIRING:

ONBOARDING:

CAREER MAPS:

SUCCESSION PLANNING:

PERFORMANCE REVIEWS:

PROMOTIONS:

EMPLOYEE ENGAGEMENT:

EMPLOYEE TURNOVER:

LEADERSHIP TURNOVER:

EMPLOYER OF CHOICE:

- How can you create partnership with Human Resources? It's critical that you engage the HR organization in Talent GPS work. Working around or avoiding the HR group will eventually kill your transition project. The more help you can get, the better.
- What works more effectively—gradual or all-at-once transition? Usually, small bites work better than big hammers. How can you grow these processes as sequential pilots and then finalize them into ongoing processes? How can you move small pieces slowly to reduce resistance and implement more thoroughly?
- What's the consistent message you'll share about why this process is important? What will it take to have success and who will you need to collaborate with? Be prepared to work with others to make a tagline to reinforce the purpose (see Appendix D Career Map to reuse the 3 Verbs and 1 noun process to build a quick and impactful purpose statement).
- Are you passionate enough to tell your own story? Take a big risk and share your own example as a model of both challenge and success. Be authentic.
- What if you don't know exactly how this is going to work? Share what you know and ask for help from others when you aren't sure.

"Build it and they will come" never works. To implement a process successfully requires engaging the stakeholders in the purpose, the transition, and the benefits. Success requires evangelism—a committed Project Sponsor and a dedicated Project Manager in partnership with stakeholders. Included in Appendix C are the following templates to help you strategize and implement the transition are:

- The Dare to Properly Manage Resource PM Process
- Talent GPS Project Charter
- Sample Project Charter demo
- Talent GPS Project Plan
- Talent GPS Transition Plan

The Talent GPS Transition: Project Charter (template Appendix C Project Charter)

The Project Charter establishes WHY the organization is investing in this process. As you look at the Project Charter template in the Appendix, you'll work through minimal project management imperatives. Here are some important concepts that will help you complete the key components of the Project Charter:

- The Project Sponsor role ensures that the project will improve the organization by either increasing revenue or driving cost from the business. The Sponsor has a strategic view. A good Project Sponsor is the single most important success factor on a project. The Project Manager role ensures that all the tasks get delegated and done in the appropriate timeframe. The Project Manager is an operational view. You can only play one of these roles. Who will be the visionary Project Sponsor for this project? Should you play this role or would it be more successful if you recruited one of your leaders to play this role?

- Who will be the Project Manager? Consider using this as a developmental opportunity for one of your high potential team members if you've decided to play the role of Project Sponsor.

- Who are the functional staff needed to do this project? What roles in your organization need to be included? Consider the following: HR, Operations, Sales, Marketing, IT, Directors, Customers (internal/external), Vendors, Purchasing and you'll likely have more. Figure out the roles you need, then put names on them: who can and will you recruit to represent these roles? These people will have work to do on the project.

- It's hard to get budget for a project like this. It's likely this will be a *guerilla* project—you'll have to figure out how to get it done with minimal budget and people busy with other things. Plan how to build small pieces in the order of most organizational need. Trying to get this project done quickly will be its downfall.

- Set emotional goals to engage stakeholders for the project: How will hiring change? Onboarding? Career Maps? Succession? Turnover?

Engagement? Use the brainstorming you did in the initial sidebar in this chapter to come up with 3-5 Big Hairy Audacious Goals (BHAG).

+ In the absence of information, people worry about what's happening and how it could threaten their status quo. You can't communicate too much. Find someone to be your 'marketing' asset to do regular communication. Tell your stakeholders early and often what you want them to know: Why (purpose), how, what, and when. Tell them the things you know and the things you aren't sure about yet. As sponsor, you own the dream and you're the best person to sell it.

+ Do you have to get approval or sign-off from anyone? What will that look like and when? Be aware of the politics and play correctly.

+ Final step: what or who are the barriers that will get in your way? What are the risks? If you can't go over, around, or under, what will you do? Listing bad things before they happen and figuring out how you'll mitigate is the work of a mature and intelligent leader.

Project Plan (Appendix C)

The Project Plan builds on the Project Charter and establishes how you'll organize the work to complete the Talent GPS transition. It's likely that you're "borrowing" people to help you, and they'll appreciate clarity around the work you need from them. The Scope Diagram in the Project Charter provides insight into the Project Plan and is an important audit that you've thought of all the tasks that need to be done.

The Project Manager will create a spreadsheet for you with all the work to be done. Each row of the spreadsheet will have a Task, Owner and Due Date. Here's a sample table:

Task	Owner	Date Due	Comments	Done
Kickoff Meeting	Lou	9/1/18	Go over charter and plan with stakeholders	√

Task	Owner	Date Due	Comments	Done
Build Job Benchmark for self	Jo	10/1/18		
Build Job Benchmark for self	Tam	10/1/18		
Build Job Benchmark for Self	Surit	10/1/18		
…etc.				
Task	Owner	Date Due	Comments	Done
Kickoff Meeting	Lou	9/1/18	Go over charter and plan with stakeholders	√
Build Job Benchmark for self	Jo	10/1/18		
Build Job Benchmark for self	Tam	10/1/18		
Build Job Benchmark for Self	Surit	10/1/18		
…etc.				

As an audit, every person's name that you put on the list of roles in the Project Charter will have tasks to do assigned to them in this table. The Project Manager will also have lots of tasks to do, and as Project Sponsor, you will as well.

The Project Manager will schedule a reminder to update the Project Plan every week, communicating status with everyone involved to keep momentum and buy-in going. Coach the Project Manager to:

+ Stay calm because busy people will push back and criticize at times.

+ Help all involved celebrate successes, even small ones.
+ Be open to others' ideas and change your approach if needed.
+ Continually explain your "why": grow engagement, reduce turnover, grow profit.

What happens if you skip this?

When was the last time you attended a workshop? What happened when it was over? What improvement did you transfer to your life or work? Chances are, you didn't have the time or energy to transfer much of what you've learned—statistics reinforce this fact. Don't let that happen with your investment in talent. It's too important to too many people.

As a great leader, your primary role is to grow those who will lead in the future. Don't get distracted by the day-to-day noise of email, drama, and churn. If your staff doesn't believe that you hold their future in trust, they won't feel engaged with the business and work. Your turnover will increase and your outcomes will decline.

Lessons Learned

+ What opportunities are now available to you that you never thought of prior to reading this book?
+ How will you prioritize your time differently based on what you've learned?
+ How will you encourage your team, peers, and leaders to be more intentional about Talent GPS so that together you can grow stellar performance?
+ When you get frustrated, and you will, what will you do to remind yourself that this is the right thing to do?
+ How will you build a community to support Talent GPS?

Make it Happen

✓ Don't just read this book – do something! Make small change and grow your ability to lead your staff to their best future while leading your own as well.

- ✓ Thank you for reading this book, and we'd love to hear from you. Email us at info@russellmartin.com .
- ✓ **Watch this video.** This video reinforces the important role you play for your talent. Thank you for investing in them. Continue to be their GPS. https://www.youtube.com/watch?v=xd1QnNBZQ2A
- ✓ Check out Appendix F for a link to the templates

Appendices

Samples, Resources & Tools

Talent GPS Roadmap

A: Talent Hacks

B: Diagnostic Assessments

- TTI Job Report
- TTI Talent (Coaching) Report
- TTI Job Benchmark Gap Report (Comparison)

C: Project Management Templates

- Project Charter
- Scope Diagram
- Transition Plan
- Project Schedule

D: Talent GPS Templates and Worksheets

- Key Accountabilities Sample
- Describe the Job
  - Behaviors (DISC)
  - Motivators
  - Competencies

- Job Benchmark
  - Sample Rankings
- Onboarding
  - S.M.A.R.T. Goals
  - All About YOU
- Career Map
  - Build Your Base
  - Current State
  - Personal Goals
  - Career Strategy
  - Gaps & Development Plan
  - Succession Plan

E: Legal Resources

F: Online Resources www.russellmartin.com/XXX

Appendix A

Talent Hacks

Top Ten

10 An engaged employee comes from the trust in a company and its leaders who value growing others throughout their careers.

9 Identify your succession candidates (see Chapter 6). Provide feedback on your choices to all your direct reports. Encourage them to do the same.

8 Encourage your direct reports to build Key Accountabilities with and for all of their direct reports. Tweak these as a team for accuracy. This will also help to create a shared appreciation for other's jobs.

7 Use Gap Reports to create Career Maps for each of your direct reports. Review these together on a regular basis.

6 Build a personal Career Map and share it with your boss and peers for feedback on a regular basis.

5 Have prizes for those of your direct reports who submit their Key Accountabilities to you. Discuss and tweak together. Create Job Benchmarks for each of their jobs. Make you Succession Plan part of your performance review (which is synched with the Career Map).

4   Start small. Create a Job Benchmark for a job you have trouble filling. Use the Job Benchmark with a Gap Report to help you identify they best candidate, then build an Onboarding Plan based on the strengths of the candidates and the gaps using the Gap Report to build a Career Map. Make a big deal about it so everyone can see what you are doing and how it changes the game. Adopt the use of Job Benchmarks and Gap Reports for future hiring.

3   Don't be afraid to go public. Secrecy degrades engagement. Be open, be honest and be factual. If you lose an employee because he or she was not chosen, remember you decided through careful consideration that he or she was not the best candidate. If they have chosen not to seek to mitigate their gaps that you discussed, it's appropriate that they move on.

2   The Gap Report for the current job of a candidate will not necessarily predict their match to the job of the Leader. The Leader choosing the pool should certainly review the person's current job Gap Report, but a more predictive Gap Report will come from comparison to the Job Benchmark of the Leader role.

1   Be very careful not to value the level of the job over the opportunity. A higher job is not always a better job. Don't be tricked by prestige or salary into taking a job that makes you crazy. Do not choose people for a position who are most like the person leaving. The candidates must be compared to the Job Benchmark based on the Key Accountabilities, not the Leader currently in the role. No one is a perfect match for a job, so comparing a potential successor to the person instead of the job would create bias the provokes a poor job fit.

Appendix B

Diagnostic Assessments

<u>Job Report</u>

Create a job benchmark from multiple experts

If the job could talk, it would clearly define the knowledge, hard skills, people skills, behavior and culture needed for superior performance. An expert's unbiased input regarding the specific requirements of the job in question has been applied to the TriMetrix® HD Job benchmarking process. The result is an evaluative report that analyzes a total of 55 separate areas. Additional feedback and suggested interview questions that pertain to each area complete this report. The following samples are just a few of the areas highlighted in the Job Report.

TTI SUCCESS INSIGHTS
DISCOVER · ENGAGE · ADVANCE · PERFORM

Key Characteristics of the Position

The position has been analyzed relative to four key characteristics. These characteristics are accountability for results, results through people, authority, and risk. Based on the responses to the questionnaire, these characteristics have been measured on a sliding scale and are illustrated by a bar graph. The scale range includes none, slight, moderate, significant, and major.

Accountability For Results: This characteristic addresses the accountability for producing measurable results in the position. This includes accountability for meeting financial, operations and/or system objectives.

None	Slight	Moderate	Significant	Major

Results through People: This characteristic address the emphasis on producing results through the efforts and cooperation of people. This characteristic is not limited to management or leadership positions. Many non-management or leadership positions in team-based organizational structures depend heavily upon the efforts and cooperation of people to produce results.

None	Slight	Moderate	Significant	Major

Authority: This characteristic addresses the level of authority that exists in the position. Evidence of authority can be found in the ability to make decisions or changes without prior approval from upper management. This characteristic is not limited to management or leadership position. In their efforts to become more responsive, many large organizations are finding it necessary to drive decision-making downward. In these organizations, many positions can be characterized by a moderate to significant amount of authority but are not considered management or leadership.

None	Slight	Moderate	Significant	Major

Risks: This characteristic addresses the inherent level of business risk or liability to the organization that exists in the position. Positions with indications of moderate, significant or major levels of inherent risk or liability to the organization may warrant the use of drug, alcohol and/or other appropriate assessments in their selection and management systems.

None	Slight	Moderate	Significant	Major

Key Characteristics The position has been analyzed relative to four key characteristics. These characteristics are accountability for results, results through people, authority, and risk. Based on the responses to the questionnaire, these characteristics have been measured on a sliding scale and are illustrated by a bar graph. The scale range includes none, slight, moderate, significant, and major.

TTI SUCCESS INSIGHTS®
DISCOVER · ENGAGE · ADVANCE · PERFORM

Hierarchy of Competencies

The competencies required for superior performance have been prioritized based on the analysis of responses to the questionnaire. The hierarchical order of the competencies represents their relative importance to each other in producing superior performance in the job.

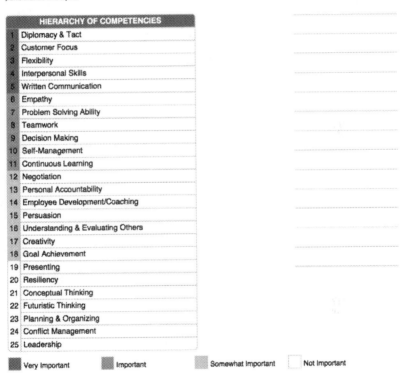

HIERARCHY OF COMPETENCIES
1 Diplomacy & Tact
2 Customer Focus
3 Flexibility
4 Interpersonal Skills
5 Written Communication
6 Empathy
7 Problem Solving Ability
8 Teamwork
9 Decision Making
10 Self-Management
11 Continuous Learning
12 Negotiation
13 Personal Accountability
14 Employee Development/Coaching
15 Persuasion
16 Understanding & Evaluating Others
17 Creativity
18 Goal Achievement
19 Presenting
20 Resiliency
21 Conceptual Thinking
22 Futuristic Thinking
23 Planning & Organizing
24 Conflict Management
25 Leadership

■ Very Important   ■ Important   ■ Somewhat Important   ☐ Not Important

Provided by:
Your Address Here
Your Phone Number Here
Your Email Address Here

Subject Matter Expert (SME) #3
Copyright © 2006-2013. Target Training International, Ltd. 4

Hierarchy of Competencies The competencies required for superior performance have been prioritized based on the analysis of responses to the questionnaire. The hierarchical order of the competencies represents their relative importance to each other in producing superior performance in the job.

Job Report

Create a job benchmark from multiple experts

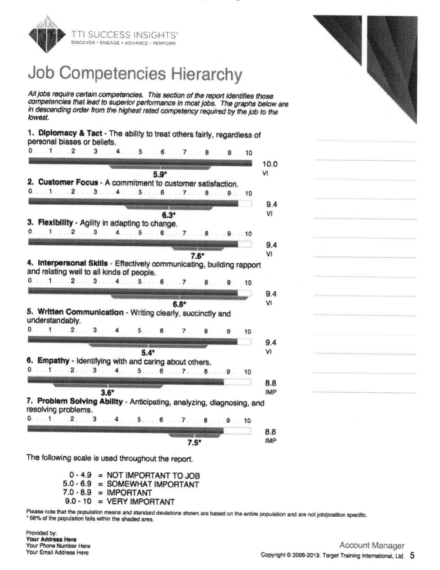

TTI SUCCESS INSIGHTS®
DISCOVER • ENGAGE • ADVANCE • PERFORM

Job Competencies Hierarchy

All jobs require certain competencies. This section of the report identifies those competencies that lead to superior performance in most jobs. The graphs below are in descending order from the highest rated competency required by the job to the lowest.

1. Diplomacy & Tact - The ability to treat others fairly, regardless of personal biases or beliefs.

0   1   2   3   4   5   6   7   8   9   10

5.9*
10.0
VI

2. Customer Focus - A commitment to customer satisfaction.

0   1   2   3   4   5   6   7   8   9   10

6.3*
9.4
VI

3. Flexibility - Agility in adapting to change.

0   1   2   3   4   5   6   7   8   9   10

7.5*
9.4
VI

4. Interpersonal Skills - Effectively communicating, building rapport and relating well to all kinds of people.

0   1   2   3   4   5   6   7   8   9   10

6.8*
9.4
VI

5. Written Communication - Writing clearly, succinctly and understandably.

0   1   2   3   4   5   6   7   8   9   10

5.4*
9.4
VI

6. Empathy - Identifying with and caring about others.

0   1   2   3   4   5   6   7   8   9   10

3.6*
8.8
IMP

7. Problem Solving Ability - Anticipating, analyzing, diagnosing, and resolving problems.

0   1   2   3   4   5   6   7   8   9   10

7.5*
8.8
IMP

The following scale is used throughout the report.

0 - 4.9	= NOT IMPORTANT TO JOB
5.0 - 6.9	= SOMEWHAT IMPORTANT
7.0 - 8.9	= IMPORTANT
9.0 - 10	= VERY IMPORTANT

Please note that the population means and standard deviations shown are based on the entire population and are not job/position specific.
* 68% of the population falls within the shaded area.

Provided by:
Your Address Here
Your Phone Number Here
Your Email Address Here

Job Competencies Hierarchy All jobs require certain competencies. This section of the report identifies those competencies that lead to superior performance in most jobs. The graphs below are in descending order from the highest rated competency required by the job to the lowest.

 TTI SUCCESS INSIGHTS®
DISCOVER · ENGAGE · ADVANCE · PERFORM

Organizational Rewards/Culture Hierarchy

This section identifies the rewards/culture system of a specific organization. Matching a person's passion to an organization that rewards that passion always enhances performance. The graphs below are in descending order from the highest rewards/culture required by the organization to the lowest.

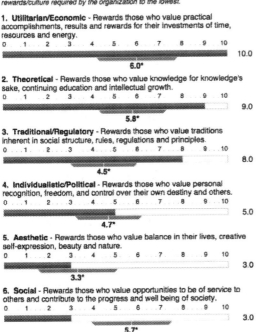

1. Utilitarian/Economic - Rewards those who value practical accomplishments, results and rewards for their investments of time, resources and energy.

0 . 1 . 2 . 3 . 4 . 5 . 6 . 7 . 8 . 9 . 10   **10.0**

6.0*

2. Theoretical - Rewards those who value knowledge for knowledge's sake, continuing education and intellectual growth.

0 . 1 . 2 . 3 . 4 . 5 . 6 . 7 . 8 . 9 . 10   **9.0**

5.8*

3. Traditional/Regulatory - Rewards those who value traditions inherent in social structure, rules, regulations and principles.

0 . 1 . 2 . 3 . 4 . 5 . 6 . 7 . 8 . 9 . 10   **8.0**

4.5*

4. Individualistic/Political - Rewards those who value personal recognition, freedom, and control over their own destiny and others.

0 . 1 . 2 . 3 . 4 . 5 . 6 . 7 . 8 . 9 . 10   **5.0**

4.7*

5. Aesthetic - Rewards those who value balance in their lives, creative self-expression, beauty and nature.

0 . 1 . 2 . 3 . 4 . 5 . 6 . 7 . 8 . 9 . 10   **3.0**

3.3*

6. Social - Rewards those who value opportunities to be of service to others and contribute to the progress and well being of society.

0 . 1 . 2 . 3 . 4 . 5 . 6 . 7 . 8 . 9 . 10   **3.0**

5.7*

* 68% of the population falls within the shaded area.

Provided by:
Your Address Here
Your Phone Number Here
Your Email Address Here

Organizational Rewards / Culture Hierarchy This section identifies the rewards/culture system of a specific organization. Matching a person's passion to an organization that rewards that passion always enhances performance. The graphs below are in descending order from the highest rewards/culture required by the organization to the lowest.

Job Report

Create a job benchmark from multiple experts

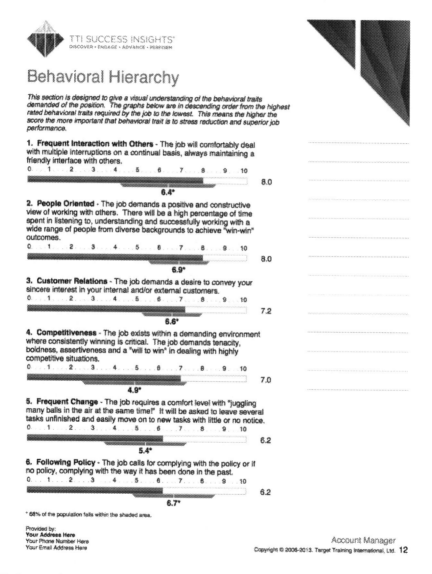

Behavioral Hierarchy This section is designed to give a visual understanding of the behavioral traits demanded of the position. The graphs below are in descending order from the highest rated behavioral traits required by the job to the lowest. This means the higher the score the more important that behavioral trait is to stress reduction and superior job performance.

TTI SUCCESS INSIGHTS®
DISCOVER · ENGAGE · ADVANCE · PERFORM

Acumen Indicators

This section identifies the acumen needed for superior performance in this position. These scores are calculated based on the world view (blue) and self view (red) required by the job. Each factor has a clarity score from one to ten and a bias indicator ranging from undervalued, neutral or overvalued for each dimension.

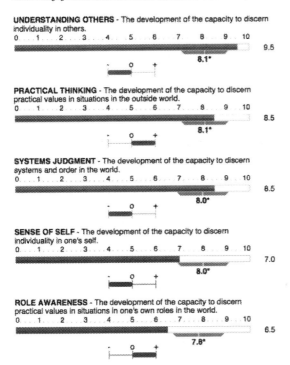

UNDERSTANDING OTHERS - The development of the capacity to discern individuality in others.

0 . . . 1 . . . 2 . . . 3 . . . 4 . . . 5 . . . 6 . . . 7 . . . 8 . . . 9 . . . 10

9.5

8.1*

PRACTICAL THINKING - The development of the capacity to discern practical values in situations in the outside world.

0 . . . 1 . . . 2 . . . 3 . . . 4 . . . 5 . . . 6 . . . 7 . . . 8 . . . 9 . . 10

8.5

8.1*

SYSTEMS JUDGMENT - The development of the capacity to discern systems and order in the world.

0 . . . 1 . . . 2 . . . 3 . . . 4 . . . 5 . . . 6 . . . 7 . . . 8 . . . 9 . . . 10

8.5

8.0*

SENSE OF SELF - The development of the capacity to discern individuality in one's self.

0 . . . 1 . . . 2 . . . 3 . . . 4 . . . 5 . . . 6 . . . 7 . . . 8 . . . 9 . . . 10

7.0

8.0*

ROLE AWARENESS - The development of the capacity to discern practical values in situations in one's own roles in the world.

0 . . . 1 . . . 2 . . . 3 . . . 4 . . . 5 . . . 6 . . . 7 . . . 8 . . . 9 . . . 10

6.5

7.8*

Provided by:
Your Address Here
Your Phone Number Here
Your Email Address Here

Account Manager
Copyright © 2006-2013. Target Training International, Ltd. **14**

Acumen Indicators This section identifies the acumen needed for superior performance in this position. These scores are calculated based on the world view (blue) and self view (red) required by the job. Each factor has a clarity score from one to ten and a bias indicator ranging from undervalued, neutral or overvalued for each dimension.

Coaching Report

A detailed look at your talent

The TriMetrix® HD Coaching Report was designed to increase the understanding of an individual's talents. The report provides insight to four distinct areas: behaviors, motivators, acumen and competencies. Understanding strengths and weaknesses in each of the four areas will lead to personal and professional development and a higher level of satisfaction.

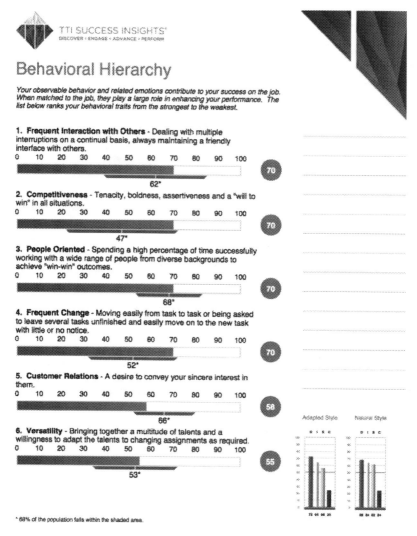

Driving Forces Graph

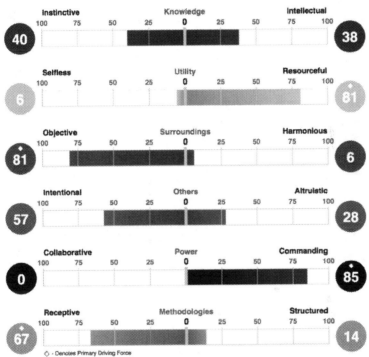

◇ - Denotes Primary Driving Force

Coaching Report

A detailed look at your talent

Checklist for Communicating Continued

This section of the report is a list of things NOT to do while communicating with Juliane. Review each statement with Juliane and identify those methods of communication that result in frustration or reduced performance. By sharing this information, both parties can negotiate a communication system that is mutually agreeable.

Ways **NOT** to Communicate

- ☐ Use gimmicks or clever, quick manipulations.
- ☐ Talk in a loud voice or use confrontation.
- ☐ Rush the decision-making process.
- ☐ Use testimonies of unreliable sources; don't be haphazard.
- ☐ Threaten, cajole, wheedle, coax or whimper.
- ☐ Make conflicting statements.
- ☐ Make promises you cannot deliver.
- ☐ Don't be haphazard.
- ☐ Make statements about the quality of her work unless you can prove it.
- ☐ Push too hard, or be unrealistic with deadlines.
- ☐ Dillydally, or waste time.
- ☐ Talk to her when you're extremely angry.
- ☐ Be vague about what's expected of either of you; don't fail to follow through.

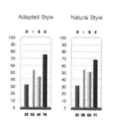

Provided by:
Your Address Here
Your Phone Number Here
Your Email Address Here

Juliane Sample
Copyright © 2006-2013. Target Training International, Ltd. **7**

Most people are aware of and sensitive to the ways with which they prefer to be communicated. Many people find this section to be extremely accurate and important for enhanced interpersonal communication. This page provides other people with a list of things to DO when communicating with the specific person.

TTI SUCCESS INSIGHTS™
DISCOVER • ENGAGE • ADVANCE • PERFORM

Checklist for Communicating

Most people are aware of and sensitive to the ways with which they prefer to be communicated. Many people find this section to be extremely accurate and important for enhanced interpersonal communication. This page provides other people with a list of things to DO when communicating with Juliane. Read each statement and identify the 3 or 4 statements which are most important to her. We recommend highlighting the most important "DO's" and provide a listing to those who communicate with Juliane most frequently.

Ways to Communicate

☐ Support your communications with correct facts and data.

☐ Give her time to verify reliability of your comments--be accurate and realistic.

☐ Give her time to verify reliability of your actions; be accurate, realistic.

☐ Support her principles; use a thoughtful approach; build your credibility by listing pros and cons to any suggestion you make.

☐ Take time to be sure that she is in agreement and understands what you said.

☐ Be sincere and use a tone of voice that shows sincerity.

☐ Give her time to be thorough, when appropriate.

☐ Make an organized contribution to her efforts, present specifics and do what you say you can do.

☐ Prepare your "case" in advance.

☐ Follow through, if you agree.

☐ Draw up a scheduled approach to implementing action with a step-by-step timetable; assure her that there won't be surprises.

☐ Make an organized presentation of your position, if you disagree.

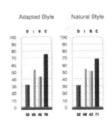

Provided by:
Your Address Here
Your Phone Number Here
Your Email Address Here

Juliane Sample
Copyright © 2006-2013. Target Training International, Ltd. 6

Similar to the example on the left, it's often just as important to understand the ways that are not effective when communicating with someone. This section of the report is a list of things NOT to do while communicating with the specific person..

Coaching Report

A detailed look at your talent

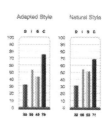

Time Wasters

This section of your report is designed to identify time wasters that may impact your overall time use effectiveness. Possible causes and solutions will serve as a basis for creating an effective plan for maximizing your use of TIME and increasing your PERFORMANCE.

Waiting For Events To Happen

Although patience may be a virtue, being pro-active allows the decision-maker to be in better control of events within their scope of influence.

Possible Causes:

* Want to affect the here and now
* Fear rushing into something will show unpreparedness
* Need for high standards inhibits getting started

Possible Solutions:

* Plan alternative solutions
* Determine most likely scenarios
* Implement a plan that best meets those needs without jeopardizing other scenarios

Seeking "All" of The Facts

Seeking "all" of the facts is thought and action of continually gathering new information and re-evaluating current information.

Possible Causes:

* Want to be certain/prepared
* Want to avoid mistakes
* Want extended time for getting tasks done

Possible Solutions:

* Set a timeline for gathering new information or evaluating old information and then take action
* Evaluate importance or risk factors to how much information is actually needed

Provided by:
Your Address Here
Your Phone Number Here
Your Email Address Here

Juliane Sample
Copyright © 2006-2013. Target Training International, Ltd. 15

This section of the report is designed to identify time wasters that may impact a person's overall time use effectiveness. Possible causes and solutions will serve as a basis for creating an effective plan for maximizing the use of time and increasing a person's performance.

Perceptions
See Yourself as Others See You

A person's behavior and feelings may be quickly telegraphed to others. This section provides additional information on Juliane's self-perception and how, under certain conditions, others may perceive her behavior. Understanding this section will empower Juliane to project the image that will allow her to control the situation.

Self-Perception

Juliane usually sees herself as being:

* Precise
* Moderate
* Knowledgeable

* Thorough
* Diplomatic
* Analytical

Others' Perception - Moderate

Under moderate pressure, tension, stress or fatigue, others may see her as being:

* Pessimistic
* Worrisome

* Picky
* Fussy

Others' Perception - Extreme

Under extreme pressure, stress or fatigue, others may see her as being:

* Perfectionistic
* Strict

* Hard-to-Please
* Defensive

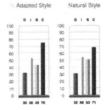

Adapted Style   Natural Style

Juliane Sample
9

A person's behavior and feelings may be quickly telegraphed to others. This section provides additional information on a person's self-perception and how, under certain conditions, others may perceive her behavior. Understanding this section will empower an individual to project the image that will allow her to control the situation.

Coaching Report

A detailed look at your talent

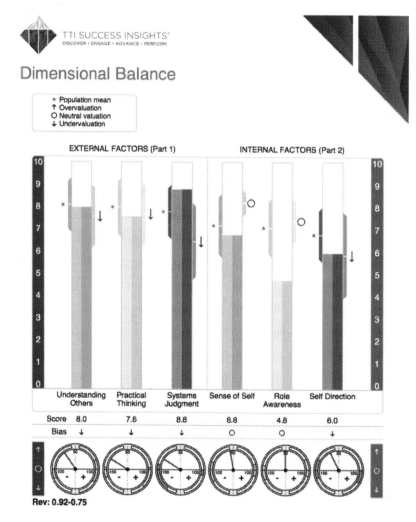

The Acumen Indicators Section is designed to help an individual truly understand themselves, how they analyze and interpret their experiences. A person's acumen, keenness and depth of perception or discernment, is directly related to their level of performance. The stronger a person's acumen, the more aware they are of their reality in both their external and internal world.

Natural and Adapted Style

Jan's natural style of dealing with problems, people, pace of events and procedures may not always fit what the environment needs. This section will provide valuable information related to stress and the pressure to adapt to the environment.

Problems - Challenges

Natural

Jan is ambitious in her approach to problem solving, displaying a strong will and a need to win against all obstacles. Jan has a tendency to make decisions with little or no hesitation.

Adapted

Jan sees no need to change her approach to solving problems or dealing with challenges in her present environment.

People - Contacts

Natural

Jan is sociable and optimistic. She is able to use an emotional appeal to convince others of a certain direction. She likes to be on a team and may be the spokesman for the team. She will trust others and likes a positive environment in which to relate.

Adapted

Jan sees no need to change her approach to influencing others to her way of thinking. She sees her natural style to be what the environment is calling for.

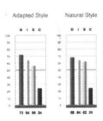

Adapted Style   Natural Style

Jan Cole

A person's natural style of dealing with problems, people, pace of events and procedures may not always fit what the environment needs. This section will provide valuable information related to stress and the pressure to adapt to the environment.

Job Benchmark

Comparing Candidates

This report compares a specific job benchmark to the results of one to five talent reports. Use the following guidelines to effectively interpret the results. When you compare a person to a specific job benchmark, you must ask yourself some very important questions with regard to the top seven competencies, the top three motivators, and the top three behaviors and the Acumen Indicators. The answers to the following questions will maximize the use of this report.

Job Competencies Hierarchy

All jobs require certain competencies. This section of the report identifies those competencies that lead to superior performance in most jobs. The graphs below are in descending order from the highest rated competency required by the job to the lowest.

1. Customer Focus - Anticipating, meeting and/or exceeding customer needs, wants and expectations.

0. . . .10. . . 20. . . 30. . . 40. . . 50. . . 60. . . 70. . . 80. . . 90. . .100

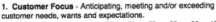

100	Job
69	*
100	Tony Block
83	Andi Porter
80	Jan Cole
100	William Sales
87	Tom Roberts

2. Personal Accountability - A measure of the capacity to be answerable for personal actions.

0. . . .10. . . 20. . . 30. . . 40. . . 50. . . 60. . . 70. . . 80. . . 90. . .100

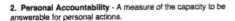
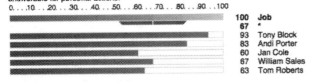

100	Job
67	*
93	Tony Block
83	Andi Porter
60	Jan Cole
67	William Sales
63	Tom Roberts

3. Goal Orientation - Setting, pursuing and attaining goals, regardless of obstacles or circumstances.

0. . . .10. . . 20. . . 30. . . 40. . . 50. . . 60. . . 70. . . 80. . . 90. . .100

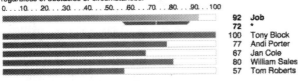

92	Job
72	*
100	Tony Block
77	Andi Porter
67	Jan Cole
80	William Sales
57	Tom Roberts

4. Interpersonal Skills - Effectively communicating, building rapport and relating well to all kinds of people.

0. . . .10. . . 20. . . 30. . . 40. . . 50. . . 60. . . 70. . . 80. . . 90. . .100

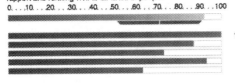

92	Job
71	*
100	Tony Block
87	Andi Porter
73	Jan Cole
93	William Sales
63	Tom Roberts

* 68% of the population falls within the shaded area.

Competencies How difficult will it be for someone to master and maintain the specific attribute for which the job is calling? If a gap exists between the job and the person, can the gap be addressed with training, or not? How cost effective will it be to train a person rather than hire someone who has already mastered the necessary attributes?

Behavioral Hierarchy

This section is designed to give a visual understanding of the behavioral traits demanded of the job and the natural behavioral style(s) of the individual(s). The graphs are in descending order from the highest rated behavioral traits required by the job to the lowest. In comparing the results in this section, it is important to note how gaps may indicate a level of stress that could be created when a person is forced to adapt behavior that is not his/her natural style.

1. Frequent Interaction with Others - The job will comfortably deal with multiple interruptions on a continual basis, always maintaining a friendly interface with others.

0. . .10. . .20. . .30. . .40. . .50. . .60. . .70. . .80. . .90. . .100

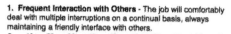

90	Job
62	*
70	Tony Block
50	Andi Porter
70	Jan Cole
90	William Sales
40	Tom Roberts

2. Competitiveness - The job exists within a demanding environment where consistently winning is critical. The job demands tenacity, boldness, assertiveness and a "will to win" in dealing with highly competitive situations.

0. . .10. . .20. . .30. . .40. . .50. . .60. . .70. . .80. . .90. . .100

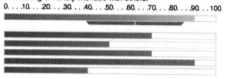

80	Job
47	*
50	Tony Block
40	Andi Porter
70	Jan Cole
100	William Sales
20	Tom Roberts

3. People Oriented - The job demands a positive and constructive view of working with others. There will be a high percentage of time spent in listening to, understanding and successfully working with a wide range of people from diverse backgrounds to achieve "win-win" outcomes.

0. . .10. . .20. . .30. . .40. . .50. . .60. . .70. . .80. . .90. . .100

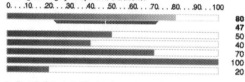

78	Job
68	*
60	Tony Block
70	Andi Porter
70	Jan Cole
75	William Sales
65	Tom Roberts

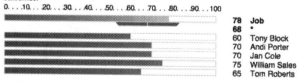

* 68% of the population falls within the shaded area.

Copyright © 2006-2015. Target Training International, Ltd. 18

Behavioral Traits How will a person feel about being required to make a major behavioral change, and how will that affect productivity?

108

Job Benchmark

Comparing Candidates

Primary Driving Forces Cluster

These graphs are based on the hierarchy of the job benchmark's driving forces in descending order from highest provided by the job to the lowest. Gaps may point to areas in the job that do not align with the persons driving forces.

1. Resourceful - People who are driven by practical results, maximizing both efficiency and returns for their investments of time, talent, energy and resources.

0....10...20...30...40...50...60...70...80...90...100

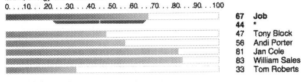

67	Job
44	*
47	Tony Block
56	Andi Porter
81	Jan Cole
83	William Sales
33	Tom Roberts

2. Commanding - People who are driven by status, recognition and control over personal freedom.

0....10...20...30...40...50...60...70...80...90...100

54	Job
49	*
47	Tony Block
43	Andi Porter
85	Jan Cole
79	William Sales
0	Tom Roberts

3. Receptive - People who are driven by new ideas, methods and opportunities that fall outside a defined system for living.

0....10...20...30...40...50...60...70...80...90...100

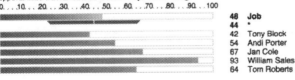

48	Job
44	*
42	Tony Block
54	Andi Porter
67	Jan Cole
93	William Sales
64	Tom Roberts

* 68% of the population falls within the shaded area.

Rewards/ Culture How will a person feel if they have to spend eight hours a day in a culture that does not reward their passion? How will a person feel if he/she has negative feelings about the built-in rewards and culture of the job?

Acumen Indicators

This section identifies the acumen needed for superior performance in this position. These scores are calculated based on the world view (blue) and self view (red) required by the job. Each factor has a clarity score from one to ten and a bias indicator ranging from undervalued, neutral or overvalued for each dimension.

UNDERSTANDING OTHERS - The development of the capacity to discern individuality in others.

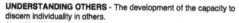

0 . . . 10 . . . 20 . . . 30 . . . 40 . . . 50 . . . 60 . . . 70 . . . 80 . . . 90 . . . 100

Score	Name
95 (-)	**Job**
81	*
80 (-)	Tony Block
86 (o)	Andi Porter
80 (-)	Jan Cole
78 (o)	William Sales
88 (+)	Tom Roberts

PRACTICAL THINKING - The development of the capacity to discern practical values in situations in the outside world.

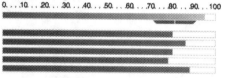

0 . . . 10 . . . 20 . . . 30 . . . 40 . . . 50 . . . 60 . . . 70 . . . 80 . . . 90 . . . 100

Score	Name
92 (+)	**Job**
80	*
92 (-)	Tony Block
74 (-)	Andi Porter
76 (-)	Jan Cole
64 (-)	William Sales
72 (-)	Tom Roberts

SYSTEMS JUDGMENT - The development of the capacity to discern systems and order in the world.

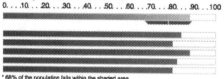

0 . . . 10 . . . 20 . . . 30 . . . 40 . . . 50 . . . 60 . . . 70 . . . 80 . . . 90 . . . 100

Score	Name
88 (-)	**Job**
78	*
84 (+)	Tony Block
80 (o)	Andi Porter
88 (-)	Jan Cole
82 (+)	William Sales
80 (o)	Tom Roberts

* 68% of the population falls within the shaded area.

Additional Consideration How are other people in the same job performing based on the results of their TriMetrix® HD Talent Report?

Appendix C

PM Templates

Scope Diagram

Project
Sponsor:

Project Charter:	

Communications Strategy (status and messaging)

Stakeholder	Goal	Frequency	Medium	Comment

Governance Strategy (approval and change requests)

Type of change (requirements, budget, scope, etc.)	Final decision makers	Consulted	Comments

Project Charter:	

Transition Plan

Task	Deliverable	Owner	Due Date	Comment

| Project Schedule: | | | | | |

Task	Task Owner	Helpers	Due	Comments	Complete

Project Charter:	Finalize PM

Business Objectives (Increase Revenue, Avoid Cost)
Primary My project will increase Revenue by providing a logical, enticing next step for our alumni and a 'influencing skills' learning solution for new students.

Secondary None

Project Objectives
- Transition the PM workshop into a viable offering including all marketing and peripheral sales
- Develop product sales for PM Templates (Project Connection?)
- Develop a portal / portfolio solution for customers who have none.
- Include Trimetrix EQ in solution to grow product sales.

Quick N' Dirty Risk:
Size (1-10 big)	2
Structure (1-10 no reqmnts)	1
Technology (1-10 new)	7
Average	3.4

Constraints	Can't move	Moves little	Negotiate
Time		X	
Cost	X		
Quality/Scope			X

RISK FACTOR	LIKELIHOOD (L, M, H)	IMPACT (L, M, H)	PREVENT BY	REACT BY
Inertia – we don't have time to finish it	L	H	Project PLAN!!!	Hit the dates
Project Platform is too complicated or no market	M	M		Eliminate this part of the scope at least for now
Project Connections is not the best solution	L	M		Leverage our own templates for sale

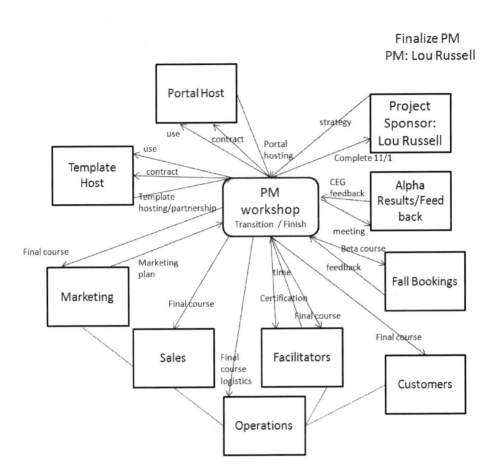

Finalize PM
PM: Lou Russell

Portal Host

Project Sponsor: Lou Russell

strategy

contract

use

Portal hosting

Complete 11/1

Template Host

use

contract

Template hosting/partnership

PM workshop
Transition / Finish

CEG feedback

Alpha Results/Feedback

meeting

Final course

Marketing plan

Marketing

Beta course

feedback

Fall Bookings

time

Final course

Certification

Sales

Final course

Final course logistics

Facilitators

Final course

Final course

Customers

Operations

Appendix C: Sample Project Charter

Project Charter:	Finalyze PM Workshop

Communications Strategy

Stakeholder	Goal	Frequency	Medium	Comment
Project Connections	Develop a mutually beneficial partnership	Monthly	Email / conf call	
Facilitators	Develop passionate facilitators for this workshop	Updates monthly starting 9/1	Email	Need to start certifying in fall sessions
Marketing/Sales/Operations	Aligned processes for all three	Need to start 9/1	Meetings/ plans created	
Portal Host	Safe, easy place to keep customer files	Need to decide by 9/1 if going ahead	Research / questions	
Fall Bookings	Great learning, positive feedback	After workshop	Normal feedback process	

Governance Strategy

Type of Change (requirements, budget, scope, etc.)	Final Decision Makers	Consulted	Comments
Budget, Scope, Requirements	Lou Russell	Brittney Helt, Pilot Students	

Appendix D

Talent GPS Templates and Worksheets

D: Talent GPS Templates and Worksheets

- Key Accountabilities Sample
- Describe the Job
- Behaviors (DISC)
- Motivators
- Competencies
- Job Benchmark
- Sample Rankings
- Onboarding
- S.M.A.R.T. Goals
- All About YOU
- Career Map
- Build Your Base
- Current State
- Personal Goals
- Career Strategy
- Gaps & Development Plan
- Succession Plan

Key Accountabilities

Lou Russell, CEO, Russell Martin & Associates

Overall Focus/Goal

Grow RMA scalability/sustainability and profit 20% per year by:

Prioritization of key accountabilities

#1 **Lead RMA resources (AVOID COSTS)** to grow the scalability and sustainability so that RMA can thrive with or without Lou. Monitor the following goals: grow facilitator bench, technology simplicity, consulting projects/reputation, strong customer relationships, systemic marketing to directors and above, strong association partnerships (ex. ATD) as well as ensure staff balance and quality of life *(50%)*.

Percentage of time spent

#2 **Teach / Present (INCREASE REVENUE)** Consult, teach and present if the client is best served and there is an ongoing relationship opportunity. Limit time for customer delivery to less than 8 days per month (including webinars) *(30%)*.

#3 **Sponsor Consulting Projects (INCREASE REVENUE)** Act as sponsor for consulting projects, leveraging the best consultants for the customer need and providing the guidelines, governance and resources necessary to be highly successful. React quickly to emergency projects *(10%)*.

Business goal

#4 **Publish / Innovate (INCREASE REVENUE)** Create new strategies, products and services to increase customer value / performance improvement *(10%)*.

Describe The Job

based on the key accountabilities

A small number (no more than 10) of subject matter experts (SMEs) should complete the following exercise. Place an X in one of the four importance categories based solely on the key accountabilities you've determined define the job. Rank each (numerically) in the last column of each of the three categories.

Section 1: Motivators (Driving Forces)					
Motivator	Very Important	Important	Somewhat Important	Not Important	Rank
Aesthetic- A passion to add balance and harmony to one's own life and protect our natural resources.					
Individualistic- A passion to achieve position and to use that position to influence others					
Social- A passion to eliminate hate and conflict in the world and to assist others.					
Theoretical-A passion to discover, systematize and analyze; a search for knowledge.					
Traditional- A passion to pursue the higher meaning in life through a defined system for living					
Utilitarian- A passion to gain return on investment of time, resources and money.					

Section 2: Behaviors					
Behavior	Very Important	Important	Somewhat Important	Not Important	Rank
Analysis of Data- Information is maintained accurately for repeated examination as required.					
Competitiveness- Tenacity, boldness, assertiveness and a "will to win" in all situations.					
Consistency- The ability to do the job the same way.					
Customer Relations- A desire to convey your sincere interest in them.					
Follow Up and Follow Through- A need to be thorough.					
Following Policy- Complying with the policy or if no policy, complying with the way it has been done.					
Frequent Change- Moving easily from task to task or being asked to leave several tasks unfinished and easily move on to the new task with little or no notice.					
Frequent Interaction with Others- Dealing with multiple interruptions on a continual basis, always maintaining a friendly interface with others.					
Organized Workplace- Systems and procedures followed for success.					
People Oriented- Spending a high percentage of time successfully working with a wide range of people from diverse backgrounds to achieve "win-win" outcomes.					
Versatility- Bringing together a multitude of talents and a willingness to adapt the talents to changing assignments as required.					
Urgency- Decisiveness, quick response and fast action.					

Continued...

Section 3: Competencies (Skills)					
Competencies	Very Important	Important	Somewhat Important	Not Important	Rank
Appreciating Others- Identifying with and caring about others.					
Conceptual Thinking- Analyzing hypothetical situations, patterns and/or abstract concepts to formulate connections and new insights.					
Conflict Management- Understanding, addressing and resolving conflict constructively.					
Continuous Learning- Taking initiative to regularly learn new concepts, technologies and/or methods.					
Creativity and Innovation- Creating new approaches, designs, processes, technologies and/or systems to achieve the desired result.					
Customer Focus- Anticipating, meeting and/or exceeding customer needs, wants and expectations.					
Decision Making- Analyzing all aspects of a situation to make consistently sound and timely decisions.					
Diplomacy- Effectively and tactfully handling difficult or sensitive					
Employee Development/Coaching- Facilitating, supporting and contributing to the professional growth of others.					
Flexibility- Readily modifying, responding and adapting to change with minimal resistance.					
Futuristic Thinking- Imagining, envisioning, projecting and/or creating what has not yet been actualized.					

Continued…

Competencies	Very Important	Important	Somewhat Important	Not Important	Rank
Goal Orientation- Setting, pursuing and attaining goals, regardless of obstacles or circumstances.					
Influencing Others- Personally affecting others actions, decisions, opinions or thinking.					
Interpersonal Skills- Effectively communicating, building rapport and relating well to all kinds of people.					
Leadership- Organizing and influencing people to believe in a vision while creating a sense of purpose and direction.					
Negotiation- Listening to many points of view and facilitating agreements between two or more parties.					
Personal Accountability- Being answerable for personal actions.					
Planning and Organizing- Establishing courses of action to ensure that work is completed effectively.					
Problem Solving- Defining, analyzing and diagnosing key components of a problem to formulate a solution.					
Project Management- Identifying and overseeing all resources, tasks, systems and people to obtain results.					
Resiliency- Quickly recovering from adversity.					
Self Starting- Demonstrating initiative and willingness to begin working.					
Teamwork- Cooperating with others to meet objectives.					

Continued...

Competencies	Very Important	Important	Somewhat Important	Not Important	Rank
Time and Priority Management- Prioritizing and completing tasks in order to deliver desired outcomes within allotted time frames.					
Understanding Others- Understanding the uniqueness and contributions of others.					

Job Benchmark

based on the outcome of the SMEs

After the SMEs have completed their individual rankings for each section and competency listed, create an aggregate using all the data. After this has been agreed on by all SMEs, candidates can be compared to the benchmark to determine their job fit.

Section 1: Motivators (Driving Forces)						
Motivator	Very Important	Important	Somewhat Important	Not Important	Rank	Candidate
Theoretical	x				1	3
Utilitarian	x				2	1
Social		x			3	6
Individualistic		x			4	4
Traditional			x		5	2
Aesthetic				x	6	5

Section 2: Behaviors

Behavior	Very Important	Important	Somewhat Important	Not Important	Rank	Candidate
Frequent Interaction with Others					1	1
People Oriented	x				2	3
Customer Relations	x				3	2
Competitiveness		x			4	6
Frequent Change	x	x			5	11
Following Policy		x			6	12
Versatility			x		7	4
Follow Up and Follow Through			x		8	5
Consistency			x		9	10
Urgency			x		10	7
Organized Workplace				x	11	9
Analysis of Data				x	12	8

Section 3: Competencies						
Competency	Very Important	Important	Somewhat Important	Not Important	Rank	Candidate
Diplomacy	X				1	1
Customer Focus	X				2	23
Flexibility	X				3	2
Interpersonal Skills	X				4	18
Self Starting	X				5	14
Appreciating Others		X			1	11
Problem Solving		X			2	12
Teamwork		X			3	3
Decision Making		X			4	13
Understanding Others		X			5	6
Continuous Learning		X			6	4
Negotiation			X		1	20
Personal Accountability			X		2	21
Employee Development/Coaching			X		3	5
Influencing Others			X		4	22
Creativity and Innovation			X		5	7
Goal Orientation			X		6	8
Time and Priority Management			X		7	24

Section 3: Competencies (continued)						
Competency	Very Important	Important	Somewhat Important	Not Important	Rank	Candidate
Resiliency				x	1	15
Conceptual Thinking				x	2	16
Futuristic Thinking				x	3	17
Planning and Organizing				x	4	10
Conflict Management				x	5	19
Leadership				x	6	9
Project Management				x	7	25

Onboarding

S.M.A.R.T. Onboarding Goals

Goal:	
Is this an immediate, short or long term goal? Anticipated completion date:	
What are the SPECIFIC elements of this goal that align with your new employee's learning needs?	
How will progress or success be MEASURED?	
What are the ACTION steps your new employee must take to achieve this goal?	
How is this goal RELEVANT to your new employee's role?	
How will this be TIME-BOUND? When and how often will you check in with your new employee?	

Note: Immediate goals = realistic for first 30 days on the job; short-term goals = realistic for the first 31-60 days on the job; and long-term goals = realistic for the first 61+ days on the job.

Onboarding

All About You Template

Full Name: _____

Preferred Name: _____

Hire Date: _____

Your Birthday: _____

Dependents (Including spouse)
- Name: _____ Birthday: _____
- Name: _____ Birthday: _____
- Name: _____ Birthday: _____

Pets: _____

Hobbies: _____

Personal/Professional Goals: _____

_____

_____

Recognition: Do you prefer to be recognized:

_____ Publicly

_____ Privately

_____ Doesn't Matter

Your Favorite Things!

Sweet snack _____

Salty snack _____

Beverage _____

Restaurant _____

Retail store/
brand _____

Collector item _____

Color _____

Flower _____

Sport/team _____

Music/Musician _____

TV Show _____

Book/Author _____

We're glad you're here!

Career Map

Step 1: Build Your Base

Follow the directions below to begin building your personal mission. This will be the foundation of your career map.

1. Start by thinking about all the activities, jobs, volunteer positions, etc that you've experienced. Write them down under "Activities/ Jobs" in the table below. You may also want to include things you haven't yet experienced, but that are of interest to you or things you've always thought about or wanted to try.

Activities/Jobs	Would Repeat	Would Not Repeat	Loved	Disliked

2. Using the list you've just created, determine which of the roles you've already done that you'd like to do again and which of those you've decided aren't a good fit for you. Mark each of these in either the *would repeat* or would not *repeat columns.*

3. Sort your list so that all the items you *would repeat* and all the things you'd like to try are grouped together.

4. Check this list for themes. Review the list of activities you aren't thrilled about and determine if there were aspects of those roles you did like and how you can leverage those moving forward. At this point, consider the results of any assessments you've completed in the past. If you know your behavioral style, take that into account. If you don't have access to these results, check out TTI Success Insights (www.ttisi.com) or begin by asking others in your organization what they believe to be your strengths.

Career Map

Step 1: Build Your Base

5. Using the information in the table above, begin writing down all the verbs you can think of that describe you and the roles you *liked* and *would repeat*.

6. Repeat step five using nouns that describe you and the roles you *liked* and *would repeat*.

7. Finally, identify all the people or groups you impact based on the roles you *liked* and *would repeat* in the table above.

Verbs	Nouns	Impact

Choose your favorite three verbs, noun and impact to write your own personal mission statement.

I _____, _____, and _____ _____ (connecting words) _____.
 (verb)   (verb)   (verb)   (noun)   *through, in, with, for* (impact)

Career Map

Step 2: Current State

Current Key Accountabilities

Consider the following question, brainstorm and add your responses below.

Questions	Answers
What do you currently *have* that you *want*?	
What do you currently *have* that you *don't want*?	
What do you currently *not have* that you *want*?	
What do you currently *not have* that you *don't want*?	

Career Map

Step 3: Personal Goals

Use the information in your brainstorming above to identify what's most important to you know and future goals.

	Priority	Current State	1 Year Goal	5 Year Goal	10 Year Goal	Retirement	Observation
Health / Well-being							
Companionship							
Financial							
Professional							
Family							
Friends							
Spiritual Growth							
Fun							
Environment							

Career Map

Step 4: Career Strategy

Considering your goals, what roles (at least three) would you like to have over the next ten years. Don't limit yourself, be open to movement (cross organizationally), various industries, etc.

	Current	1 Year	5 Years	10 Years
Job				
Company				
Job				
Company				
Job				
Company				
Job				
Company				
Job				
Company				

Career Map

Step 5: Gap & Development Plan

Considering the roles listed in step 4 and your talent what must you develop to be considered for these jobs? Be most specific for the roles between 1-5 years.

Current	Growth Needed	Outcome
1 Year	Growth Needed	Outcome
5 Years	Growth Needed	Outcome
5+ Years	Growth Needed	Outcome

Career Map

Step 6: Succession Strategy

How quickly can you replace yourself? Who are your candidates and what needs to be done for at least two people to be ready to replace you?

Candidate	Priority	Strengths	Growth Needs	Notes

Appendix E

Legal Resources

The 10 Employment Laws Every Manager Should Know	http://www.thehrspecialist.com/2783/The_10_Employment_Laws_Every_Manager_Should_Know.hr?cat=tools
Top 10 Legal Issues For Employers In 2016	http://www.mondaq.com/unitedstates/x/457778/employee+rights+labour+relations/Top+10+Legal+Issues+For+Employers+In+2016
Top 10 Legal Challenges Employers Will Face in 2016	http://www.eremedia.com/tlnt/what-are-hr-pros-asking-about-heres-one-top-10-list/
Top 10 Issues That Concern And Trouble HR Professionals	http://www.hrexaminer.com/social-medias-real-legal-issues/
Social Media's Real Legal Issues	http://www.inc.com/encyclopedia/human-resources-management-and-the-law.html
Human Resources Management and the Law	https://www.amazon.com/Practitioners-Guide-Legal-Issues-Organizations-ebook/dp/B00YCAW7N2/ref=sr_1_2?ie=UTF8&qid=1473529260&sr=8-2&keywords=HR+legal+issues

Practitioner's Guide to Legal Issues in Organizations by Chester Hanvey and Kayo Sady Legal and Regulatory Issues in Human Resources Management (Contemporary Human Resource Management Issues Challenges and Opportunities) By Ronald R. Sims Jr. and William I. Sauser	https://www.amazon.com/Regulatory-Management-Contemporary-Challenges-Opportunities/dp/1623968410/ref=sr_1_5?ie=UTF8&qid=1473529260&sr=8-5&keywords=HR+legal+issues
Dealing With Problem Employees: How to Manage Performance & Personal Issues in the Workplace by Amy Delpo and Lis Guerin	https://www.amazon.com/Dealing-Problem-Employees-Performance-Workplace-ebook/dp/B0153VIED0/ref=sr_1_9?ie=UTF8&qid=1473529260&sr=8-9&keywords=HR+legal+issues
Essentials of Personnel Assessment and Selection

by Scott Highhouse and Dennis Doverspike | https://www.amazon.com/s/ref=sr_pg_2?rh=i%3Aaps%2Ck%3AHR+legal+is-sues&page=2&keywords=HR+legal+issues&ie=UT-F8&qid=1473529260 |

Appendix F

Online Resources

Visit the Talent GPS site:

https://tinyurl.com/muj4gfl

AUTHOR BIOGRAPHY

Lou Russell is Duchess / Director of Learning at Russell Martin & Associates, a Moser Consulting company headquartered in beautiful Indianapolis. As an executive consultant, speaker and author, she channels her passion to create growth in companies by growing their people. Lou inspires greatness in leadership, projects, and teams. She is the author of seven popular books on IT, Leadership and Project Management including 10 Steps to Successful Project Management featuring the Three Pigs. Lou blends her writing with practical techniques so you can grow your capacity quickly. Encouraged by Lou's upbeat and practical style, you'll leave with new tools and renewed hope. You will be laughing, participating, and challenged. Most importantly to Lou, you will learn. She can be reached at info@russellmartin.com.

Michelle Baker has been a dynamic Talent Development leader, facilitator, consultant and champion of workplace learning for nearly 20 years, having developed and facilitated learning experiences to thousands of professionals on six continents, and whose work has been recognized by Training Magazine (Training Top 125 - 2016, 2017). She is a contributing columnist for TD Magazine and a sought-after speaker at industry conferences and events. She is an active ATD member and has served on the Board of Directors with the Association for Talent Development – Central Indiana Chapter (ATD-CIC) since 2013, currently leading the chapter as President. Michelle has also been the voice of the popular phase(two) learning blog (www.phasetwolearning.com) since 2011, reaching thousands of Human Resources, Training and Talent Development professionals each month. The blog, focused on results-driven onboarding and creative talent development strategies, has been recognized as a Top 20 Learning

& Development blog (Clarity Consultants) and a Top 50 Most Socially-Shared Learning & Development Blog (CMOE). She can be reached at michelle@phasetwolearning.com.

Brittney Helt is a Communications & Learning Development Professional in the San Diego, CA area. She is one of those people that has boundless energy and NO fear. She takes pride in her ability to proficiently manage relationships and build networks. Brittney enjoys inspiring and guiding groups to accomplish their goals. Prior to starting her own practice, she was the Client Advocate at Russell Martin & Associates for seven years, which is where she fell in love with the learning and development field. She currently works with small businesses and consultants to help create a seamless user experience for their clients. She does this by organizing the company's internal project and priority management, communication, and logistics. This allows the client interaction to be high quality and lets the client focus on growing people. She is an active ATD member, including leadership stints in the Central Indiana Chapter (ATD-CIC). She is an expert of using TTI Success Insights diagnostic assessments, like the ones in this book, to improve organizational performance. She can be reached at bbhelt@gmail.com.

Printed in the United States
By Bookmasters